The Insider's Guide
to the
Teacher Interview

The Insider's Guide
to the
Teacher Interview

Bill Kresse
and
Mike Vallely

Published by

The Resource for Teacher Interview Preparation

The Insider's Guide to the Teacher Interview

For questions about reproduction, special quantity ordering discounts or presentations by the authors, please email info@thEDUedge.com or refer to additional contact information provided at theEDUedge.com.

Printed in the United States of America.

ISBN: 978-0-9835773-0-0
Library of Congress Control Number: 2011943874

The Insider's Guide to the Teacher Interview is also available in audiobook and e-book versions through multiple outlets. Visit theEDUedge.com for more information.

Join The EDU Edge Facebook, Twitter and blog communities for more insider tips and coaching.

Cover design: Kathy Rogers (K.Corff Design)
Photos of the authors: Bogdan Fundalinski (Fundalinski Studios)

Dedicated to the teaching candidate who is persistent in their pursuit of the opportunity to inspire, engage and prepare future generations.

The Insider's Guide
to the
Teacher Interview

Contents

Introduction

We created The EDU Edge (pronounced "ee-dee-you", yep just like the prefix to all those education classes you have just finished) to help you land the teaching job of your dreams. We can't guarantee you'll get the job, but we know that if you spend some time reading this text and practicing our strategies, you will be able to significantly increase your performance in the teaching interview process. We have gathered insider information and best practices from partners in school administration from around the country to help you succeed.

We met at Cornell University in 1999 while working on our Ph.D.s in school administration and have now collectively spent dozens of years running hiring committees and selecting teachers for schools. Along the way we have seen a lot of talent fail to secure the teaching job they wanted because they were caught off guard, like deer in the headlights.

Schools are not businesses. They use specialized techniques for selecting teachers and you had

Schools are not businesses. They use specialized techniques for selecting teachers and you had better be ready for them.

better be ready for them. Unfortunately, your collegiate career center is not going to get you ready for positions in education. They need to prepare many students for a variety of different career interviews. Consequently, career centers tend to focus on general guidelines and attempt to apply them to many different fields. This leaves students heading off in search of teaching careers unprepared for the unique formats they are about to face when interviewing with schools.

We are here to give you the specifics, 'the insider scoop' on what happens in the teacher interview process and how to succeed at it. We believe that your interview skills should not undermine or delay your chances of being selected to teach the next generation of young people.

Despite our experiences, you will never find us claiming to be interviewing aces blessed with some magical skill at interviewing. In fact, we have been right where you are. We have struggled in interviews and have experienced the frustration of being turned down for jobs in education. We have learned a lot along the way and would like to save you from the obstacles we encountered. The insider information and strategies in this book will give you 'the edge' over other candidates.

This resource is designed to be a quick read for the busy teaching candidate. We know you need this information in an efficient and accessible format. Just spend a little time with us and you will significantly improve you comfort level and opportunity for success at your next teacher interview.

Now let's get to work!

Bill & Mike

The EDU Edge ™

Get the edge. Get the job.

After years of leading hiring committees, Bill Kresse and Mike Vallely established The EDU Edge (pronounced "ee-dee-you") to make life easier for aspiring teachers by providing insider tips to navigate the interview process. Get more insider information and keep up-to-date with the latest resources from The EDU Edge by joining our Twitter®, Facebook® and blog communities.

Insider Edge Note

This book includes 'Insider Edge Notes" which are special points of information you will only get from our network of insiders at The EDU Edge.

Insider Edge Doc

This book and its appendix also include 'Insider Edge Docs' which are authentic documents being used in districts across the country to hire teachers. The collection of Insider Edge Docs also includes checklists to help you get ready for interviews.

Know someone else headed into teaching?
Share this book in a variety of formats!

Audiobook at CD Baby®, iTunes®, and Amazon MP3®.

E-book at Kindle®, Nook®, iBook®, SONY Reader®, Kobo®, and Copia®

Links to these outlets and more at:
theEDUedge.com

Chapter

2

What Schools and Districts are Looking For

A large part of getting the job involves understanding what schools and the people inside them are looking for when hiring new teachers. Research shows over and over again that the most important factor in improving student achievement is the teacher. This means that committees are focused on hiring those specific types of teachers that they think will have an impact on student achievement. Whether you agree with the assumptions of these committees or not, knowing who this highly sought after brand of teacher is, will give you a leg up on convincing the committee that you are the candidate to hire.

You should know that all of us- principals, superintendents and teachers on the interview teams are looking for:

- A professional teacher who likes working with children and young adults.
- Someone who has good interpersonal and people skills.
- A teacher who is knowledgeable about the art and science of teaching as well as the content of their discipline.

- And, so important is a person who is reflective and has an interest in constantly growing as an educator- someone who is intrinsically driven to become a master teacher.

We are also looking for other things like:
- Someone who is organized.
- Someone with good ethics and will present a positive model for children.
- A professional who believes that they can make a difference in a child's life through their teaching.

And don't forget the parents and the community representatives who may be present during the interview process. They are typically looking for:
- A professional who will impress and put parents at ease.
- Someone who can be trusted to use good judgment and who will not embarrass themselves or the school.
- An adult who is eager to be a part of the school and involve themselves in the community.
- Someone who will welcome parent concerns, questions and suggestions.

To boil it down, every adult on the interview committee wants a teacher that they would be excited to have teaching their own children or grandchildren. From their perspective they want, and their kids deserve, only the best.

But before you get the job, you have to get the interview. So let's tackle that next!

How to Get the Interview

For most aspiring teachers, getting the interview seems to be the most difficult obstacle to overcome. We have a few recommendations on this issue.

Recommendation number one: Sub, Sub, Sub! The best way to get an interview for a teaching position is to get to know people and to gain contacts. And, the best way to do that is to be a substitute teacher. Most schools and districts are constantly looking for substitutes. Getting on to their substitute teaching list and into their call system is most often a formality. Decide where you are interested in subbing and call the personnel department for more information.

Subbing is not only a highly useful avenue to eventually get the job you want, it also pays the bills while you are waiting. In many states and school districts, the time you spend subbing may help you to accrue time credits and positively affect your initial date of service in the state pension system. In the case of long-term assignments, it may count as time toward earning tenure in the district should they permanently hire you for the position you are serving as a substitute for or for another permanent position.

The educational community is close-knit and a small one. If you sub, you are able to get to know the department chair in your discipline and the other teachers in the school. Trust us, from our experience this goes a long way when hiring!

This is how it works: The teachers in the schools know when a job is going to become available long before anyone else. If the teachers in the department already know and like you, they lobby for you to get an interview. Next, who makes up the interview committees? Those same teachers. In that role, they again wind up lobbying for you to get the position. In teaching, being a familiar face is a plus on your side. So we encourage you in the strongest terms to sub, sub, sub. And when you do, make friends and get to know the teachers in the school.

▮▮▮ Insider Edge Note

In addition to getting to know the teachers in the school, introduce yourself to the principal and assistant principal. Being flexible and demonstrating a willingness to go above and beyond can help your personal goal of securing full-time employment. Not only will they call you back to sub on a regular basis, when the administration sees a job come up and you have been a positive force, they will put you in the candidate pool immediately or will lobby the district office to add you to the candidate pool. Even if the principal doesn't have a job available, if you have established a relationship, you can still ask them to put a good word in for you if a job in a neighboring school district opens up. Believe us, these people talk and their talk goes a long way in hiring.

When you are subbing, every day and every single thing you do is an interview. Be sure you dress the part and do everything to put your best foot forward at every moment. You will be watched constantly to see how you respond to difficult situations, the effort and attention to detail you put into even the most routine of tasks and whether you are willing to go above and beyond to assist students and the school.

While subbing, school administrators are also watching to determine who the true "you" is. Is it someone who will only take care of the basics once hired or are you someone who has an internal motor that, regardless of the praise or consequence, is always going to be working to maximize student learning? Are you someone who is going have a positive outlook and be willing to adjust to new expectations as they arise or are you someone who is going to stagnate and create negative energy in the school culture?

> *The challenge of being a substitute teacher is that there are no moments off from being appraised...[however] you will quickly realize that you are being given a great inside track for establishing yourself as an up and coming talent among the people who do the hiring*

The challenge of being a substitute teacher is that there are no moments off from being appraised. In addition, the life of a substitute often differs from that of a full-time teaching position. You have to remember that sub placements will not mirror an actual teaching position. Students and colleagues view and respond to you differently. From our experience, individuals sometimes become discouraged as a result. Do not become frustrated by mistaking a substitute experience with that of a permanent, full-time teaching position. If you can get past the hurdles of working as a sub, you will quickly realize that you are being given a great inside track for establishing yourself as an up and coming talent among the people who do the hiring.

Recommendation number two: Put your best self forward, everywhere! We find that many candidates these days are not attending to how they are representing themselves on the internet and everywhere else that an employer or community members might be able to research you. Make sure you are who you want to be when participating in the fishbowl called the worldwide web. Trust us, it makes a significant difference.

Think your transcripts, police record and references are the only source of information hiring committees will use to check your background? School districts will research you with Google, Yahoo, Bing, Twitter, Facebook, etc. Make sure that your Internet persona is an accurate reflection of who you are as a teaching professional. Questionable behavior, language, pictures, discussions and other public interaction via the internet that reflects poorly upon you can quickly eliminate you as a candidate. The private discussion you think you are having with friends about your student teaching placement or cooperating teacher is not so private- even with privacy settings at their fullest. The rule of thumb is this: when writing anything in electronic communication or social media, from email to Twitter to Facebook and so on, do not write it unless you are comfortable with the entire world viewing it, including all of your references and potential employers.

Take a moment to be sure that your outgoing voicemail message reflects positively upon you. Schools looking to hire you want to hear a professional on the other end of the line, not a quirky, "you know what to do at the beep." In addition, be sure that anytime you are out there on the job market (and frankly anytime at all), you are answering the phone in a professional manner. Do not pick up a cell phone unless you are in surroundings that will allow for a safe and sedate conversation to take place. When you pick up the phone, be sure to answer by saying, "Hello, this is Jennifer Miller speaking." Answering your phone with "Yep", "Yo, who's calling" or "Talk to me" is not going to send the right message to an employer.

Recommendation number three: Consider a teaching assistant or teacher aide position to start if you are unable to find a teaching position.
As we have stated, subbing is an option that gets you in the door, gaining contacts and meeting people who can help you in your goal of securing a full time teaching position. But another idea that is often overlooked is taking a teaching assistant or teacher aide position in the district of your choice. Many people don't even consider this as an option, perhaps because they see it as beneath them, but we feel that this is a big mistake.

When times are tough and the teaching positions are limited, working as a teaching assistant or aide has become a legitimate and smart option. We have personally seen dozens of examples where individuals with teaching degrees have taken a teaching assistant position and then jumped into the next available teacher position in that district. The same thing happened as if I they had been a substitute teacher. They:

- took advantage of their opportunity
- proved their competence, value and talent
- interacted with the teachers and administration who got to know and like them

and then voila, they were in the candidate pool and being recommended for the available position.

Yes, many times these positions pay a lot less than a full time teaching position would, but they do come with benefits and most importantly, opportunity. They also provide daily employment at the same location each day. Finally, we have never seen a perfect teacher who was firing on all cylinders right out of college. Everyone needs time to grow and hone their practice. Like subbing, these positions provide great opportunities to hone your skills.

As teacher aide and assistant positions have less to do with basic student supervision and are increasingly oriented toward instructional support over the past fifteen years, we have seen more and more examples of students right out of teaching schools taking these positions as a pathway to full time teaching positions. They also provide a great insider view of how schools operate with less pressure while you are getting acclimated to working in an educational workplace. This understanding and ease with school operations will come in handy at interview time.

If you feel there is a stigma attached to working as an aide or assistant, get with the times and get over it. While you are sitting by the phone day after day waiting for the chance for a mere interview, your competition is working as a teacher assistant proving themselves and making contacts. They are also earning wages, benefits and possibly service credits toward a pension. They are doing what it takes to get 'the edge' in landing a teaching position.

Insider Edge Note

Never turn down an interview! Every interview experience you can put yourself through is going to make you a stronger and more confident interviewer. This book describes almost everything you could imagine encountering in an interview, but there is nothing that compares to being in the room with a committee or conducting a "live" teaching demonstration.

We frequently see candidates who turn down interviews for districts that require too far of a commute or who turn down interview opportunities at teacher recruitment events for school districts that would require them to relocate altogether. Put your name in the hat for any and all of these opportunities to interview. Each interview you receive will be an opportunity to gain experience and refine your skills for that job that you really do want.

We have also seen candidates turn down interviews for "high needs" school districts, districts that have fewer resources or for positions at private schools where the salary and benefits were lower than public schools. This is a mistake for a number of reasons. First, these candidates are missing out on invaluable interview experience. Secondly, these individuals may have discovered more about the people that make up the school community or position and realized that they judged the book incorrectly by its cover. We know many teachers who did not anticipate teaching in the setting they presently work. However, somehow they fell in love with it and now could not be dragged away with a team of a hundred horses. And finally, you have no idea what the hiring season will bring. You may not catch that big fish you have been trawling for and end up unemployed. Meanwhile your competition may have accepted one of the teaching jobs you considered undesirable and are building up useful on-the-job experience that will make them very attractive to those big fish when that dream job surfaces.

Recommendation number four: If you are still student teaching or are about to do your student teaching when reading this book, please take this opportunity seriously and do the best that you can each and every day while serving as a student teacher. We cannot stress enough that your search for the job of your dreams starts the first day of student teaching. On this day you will begin forming who you are as a teacher, begin honing your pedagogical skills, classroom management, and assessment knowledge. You will begin building a reputation with students, teachers, and administration in your cooperating school and, of course, this reputation (positive or negative) will spill outside that school by word of mouth. And obviously, you want what is said about you and your teaching ability to be positive and glowing. Moreover, on your first day of student teaching, you also start building your resume, your letters of reference, and your portfolio.

Make sure that you are snapping photos (with permission of course) and keeping copies of all the lessons and all the quality student work that your students produce. And make sure that you are doing everything that you can to have your cooperating teacher, collegiate advisor, etc. see you as a positive force in the classroom and in the school. Because at the end of your student teaching experience, you will want to ask your cooperating teacher and your college advisor for letters of recommendation. These documents will be integral pieces to your portfolio and overall interview package. In essence, make your short stay at the school special and make yourself into a student teacher that really sticks in the minds of all those around you.

Insider Edge Note

If at all possible, be sure your cooperating teacher provides you with a letter of reference that offers specific examples of your strengths. Even the finest sentiments put in generic fashion can deflate the value of a letter of reference. Ask your cooperating teacher to provide concrete examples of lessons, responses to situations or initiatives that you carried out to illustrate the qualities they are describing. These examples will verify that the cooperating teacher has worked closely with you and will also help committee members to picture you as someone who has already succeeded in the classroom instead of someone who just wants to be there someday!

Chapter

4

Cover Letter and Resume Advice

First, let's tackle a common question: what is the difference between a CV and resume? The general answer is length, purpose, and content. Resumes are characterized by brevity. They are a one to two page summary of your education, skills and work experience. CV's are longer and more detailed. They are a minimum of two pages and contain detailed explanations of previous academic and professional work. The CV includes educational and academic background about you as well as teaching, research experience, publications, presentations, awards, honors, affiliations and other details. A CV is used primarily in the United States when applying for academic, education, scientific or research positions.

Generally, we recommend that you:

- Start your Resume or CV with three to four bullet points that provide the highlights of your qualifications to catch the eye of the reviewer.
- Use a chronological approach as opposed to a functional approach.[1]

---

[1] There are three basic formats for resumes/CVs: chronological, functional, and a combination of the two. Chronological list your employment experience in reverse chronological order, starting with your most recent position and working backward in time. Functional resumes emphasize your skills, strengths, and accomplishments.

- Write simple and specific sentences.
- Be specific about your past work and accomplishments.
- Avoid language that generalizes.
- Do not write in the first or third person.
- And finally, do not write in paragraphs. Reviewers have very limited time to scan these documents and they will skip your CV if it is not efficient to read.

Insider Edge Note

While the terminology tends to be used somewhat interchangeably, we find that most K-12 educators are using a hybrid of a resume and a CV, which includes most of the structure of the traditional CV, but does not go beyond two pages. It includes an increased level of description, but does not read as a narrative such as collegiate level CV's. This allows potential employers to quickly make their way through the CV while at the same time understanding the nature of the work or accomplishment in each area. We think using this hybrid approach is advisable. Even if you are newer to the field, a two-page document with a high level of detail on your academic, related professional experiences, presentations, awards and affiliations is a good idea.

The good news is that you are developing your cover letter and CV at the right point in history. Editing and putting these documents together is easier than ever. There are a plethora of websites and software applications that will help you to build visually pleasing cover letters and CVs.

Because most word processing applications come with templates built right into them and because there is such easy access to the tools needed to build an attractive looking cover letter and vitae, there has been a shift in the game. We believe that the following issues become important in being sure your cover letter and CV get you a teaching interview and support your candidacy during the process.

First, all cover letters and CV's will look sharp, so you cannot afford to slip up on this front. Get a clean and crisp looking format. Use high quality printing and paper for all submissions. We suggest an off-white paper. This provides some personality while still offering an easy read. Some paper colors get too dark making the print difficult for a reviewer reading hundreds of resumes. Darker papers can provide problems when it comes to photocopying your resume for a committee and can attach a gloomy feeling to your candidacy. The weight of your paper should be somewhere in the 24 to 32lb. range. Taking these steps may not get you in the door, but if you falter here, you can be sure yours will be tossed to the side.

Second, be sure your documents are free of any spelling, punctuation, grammatical errors and awkward clauses. Because everyone's documents these days look so good, these types of things stick out more than ever. Given that it is so easy to generate these documents, it becomes that much more difficult for a potential employer to understand how you could have possibly let an error slip through. It becomes a reflection on your attention to detail. And, as educators there is additional judgment laid upon these types of things because you will be charged with developing these skills in your students. We know of countless examples of hiring

> *... as educators there is additional judgment laid upon [your attention to detail] because you will be charged with developing these skills in your students.*

teams that refused to interview candidates because of errors in their documents. Yes, even coaching, music, art and math positions! We have even seen cases where candidate searches that were initially viewed as a 'done deal' in the favor of a particular candidate have been turned upside down because the favored candidate submitted documents that were poorly composed or edited.

Finally, when you have read a document through so many times, you become numb to even the most obvious errors. Have as many people as possible look over your documents. Every read helps to increase the possibility that you will catch errors. If you are still connected to a collegiate environment, find the campus writing center and drop in to see if they can review your resume. Career centers usually have a resume review service, but we advise you to be careful. These centers often have to service students headed into a myriad of professions and they lean towards formats and language that is very general or that work in business. You are going into teaching. You want a cover letter and CV that will give you the edge in education-specific job search scenarios.

> *You are going into teaching. You want a cover letter and CV that will give you the edge in education-specific job search scenarios.*

Again, while having a cover letter and resume without errors does not mean you will get an interview or job, materials with mistakes will almost certainly mean that you are not going to be considered, so take editing and review of the smallest details seriously.

The order and what is and is not included in your CV are also important decisions. We recommend that all CV's begin with an abbreviated summary of your most important qualifications to catch the reader's attention. This should only be three to four bulleted items that list your years of experience, degrees, and most significant accolades.

Next you have the choice of listing experience or education. For most people right out of school with little teaching experience, the choice will be listing their educational background. If you are right out of school, you almost always should list your GPA. If you do not list it, employers assume it was disastrous. Even with a poor GPA, sometimes you can show your strength in your area of study by listing the GPA specific to your major. List your GPA's for your graduate degrees as well if they are above 3.5. While they carry less weight, they do give an indication that you took your studies seriously. If you have been in the working world for more than five years it is not necessary to list your GPA, however, if it was a GPA at or above 3.5 continue to list it regardless of how long you have been working as it is something that can help you.

If you are still in school while reading this book, please, please do anything you can to keep your GPA up. It may seem like there is no connection between your GPA and ability to inspire young minds, but employers use this as a telltale sign of your intellectual ability and work ethic. Whether it is fair or not, in education circles, there is an unspoken assumption that in order to lead students, you need to have been a relatively successful student yourself. Do not underestimate the power of the GPA when it comes to applying for teaching positions.

> *Whether it is fair or not, in education circles, there is an unspoken assumption that in order to lead students, you need to have been a relatively successful student yourself. Do not underestimate the power of the GPA when it comes to applying for teaching positions.*

If you were on an academic scholarship or part of an honors program, be sure this is listed as a part of your degree details. If you are newer to education, you have to be sure that all experiences working with young people are a part of your CV. Whether it is subbing, working in a summer camp or even collecting data in schools for a graduate professor, get it listed in your CV.

When describing your work experiences, leadership roles are valuable and important to list. Professional and educational fraternal memberships are good to list toward the conclusion of your CV. They demonstrate that you are truly interested and committed to the field. They also reflect an intrinsic interest in continually refining your teaching knowledge base and skills. If you have any published research, individual or group, or have presented, be sure these find their way into your CV as well.

Selection of references is something that is often times approached too casually by teaching candidates. Be sure to list at least two references that have directly supervised you while you have been working with students. Candidates will sometimes lean toward listing friends or coworkers because they feel the closest with this people and believe they will say the kindest things about them. There is also a tendency to list supervisors who they have worked for longer, but in a job that was not related to working with children. Those doing the hiring give these types of references much less weight compared to actual school administrators or others who have had the task of formally evaluating a candidate's progress as a teacher or student teacher.

However, not all candidates have the same situations and will not necessarily be able to have building administrators listed as references. Use the following hierarchy chart to determine how to select and list references when applying for a teaching position. Start at the top and work your way down until you have four to five references. If you do not have a reference that fits one of the categories, skip that category and keep working your way down.

Fig. 4.1 Hierarchy of References for Teaching Candidates

Quality Rank	Type of Reference
1	supervising principal
2	supervising assistant principal
3	student teaching supervisor
4	cooperating teacher from student teaching experience
5	department lead teacher
6	undergraduate/graduate professor
7	supervisor from setting not related to working with students
8	fellow teacher who has not supervised you
9	co-worker from setting not related to working with students
10	individuals who have not worked with you.

While it is important to respect the hierarchy above as much as possible, do not select a reference just because they rank high on this chart. We have encountered teaching candidates who have listed a school principal as a reference but when the principal was actually called for that reference they either did not remember the candidate or when pressed by the interviewer making the call, it became obvious that the principal really did not personally experience the work of that individual. Either outcome is not positive.

Don't s-t-r-e-t-c-h references. Or in other words, don't cite a reference that you think might look better but in the end may sacrifice the personal connection and details of what you truly bring to the table as a potential teacher in the school contacting the reference. The EDU Edge rule of thumb is to pass on a reference listed higher on our chart if they did not work with you on a regular basis and cannot comment (in a moment's notice) on your professionalism and the quality of your work.

Going along with the idea that it's crucial that your references know you and your instructional performance well, be sure to thank each of your references with a handwritten note. And do not just do this one time. Your search may span months or even a year. You may relocate or decide to look for a position in another school after a few years. As time goes by, it becomes increasingly important that you communicate periodically with references you have not worked with in the recent past to be sure they are aware they are still listed as a reference for you. As we have stated, your reference's ability to describe specific events or examples that illustrate your strengths help to build confidence and credibility in the eyes of the school administrator completing the reference review check. These recollections can fade over time so it is your job to keep the memories fresh in the minds of your references.

You can help to create mental markers by staying in touch with references. A hand-written note is just one example of a personal and efficient way to do this. We suggest that candidates make some sort of contact with references two to three times a year. This may sound labor intensive, but make it simple and easy. 'Staying in touch' can be everything from a phone call, to a quick email, or a short postcard. Let them know about your progress and thank them again for the experience you had working with them. Thank them again for being a reference. Another suggestion is to use holidays as an opportunity to send them a card wishing them the best. Yes, you are sending them a warm holiday message, but you are also creating the aforementioned mental marker.

> ### Insider Edge Note
>
> List your references right at the end of your CV. Provide their name, position, phone and email address if possible. Don't make reviewers go searching around for your references or obtain them "upon request." We believe that you should not make this into a scavenger hunt for your potential employer. We know of school administrators who refuse to pull a resume from the pile for the sole reason that they do not have the time to track down references needed for their district's prescreening procedures.

Now let's talk about cover letters. Here are some bread and butter basics when writing a cover letter:

- The paper should match the paper you use for your CV (see suggestions above for quality of CV paper).
- Send the original letter with name signed in blue.
- Use perfect grammar.
- Make sure that there are no typos or misspelled words.
- Never use impersonal greetings i.e. To Whom It May concern, Dear Madam, Dear Sir, etc.. Call the school and find out the person and the person's title to which the letter should be addressed.
- Keep the cover letter short; one page, with about three paragraphs, including your opening.
- Be sure your letter is specific to the position, district, and building you are applying to.

We recommend that you express the following in your cover letter:

- Your interest in the position.
- A very brief summary of your education or experiences.
- A very brief summary of the skills that you possess.
- Why you would be a good fit for the open position.
- How they can get in touch with you at a moment's notice.

▌▌▌ Insider Edge Note

Many candidates will feel the need to write an extensive narrative with their entire background and educational philosophy in their cover letter. Often times we'll see cover letters spanning more than one page. The cold hard reality is that cover letters rarely get read in their entirety. Schools usually have thirty to forty application packets to sift through, if not hundreds. When you write an extensive cover letter you are opening yourself up to the possibility of saying the wrong thing, grammatical errors, or obscuring the most important information you want to relay. A shorter cover letter is more likely to be read in its entirety and less likely to contain an error. Use a shorter letter and focus on making those words you do use power and professional.

Be sure that your cover letter and CV share the same fonts, paper and format so the employer knows that you have thought things through and are well organized. While a little bit of style can be useful, particularly in teaching jobs where creativity is necessary, too much creativity or flowery formatting can detract from your content.

There are those in the field who will tell you not to drop names and connections in your cover letter as this can sometimes been seen as inappropriate. However, our position is not quite as strong. If you learned of the position or are interested in the organization because of someone who is well regarded with the school community or at least well regarded by the leadership, this could be an asset in helping you to get noticed. But you have to phrase your connection in a manner that is gentle. Focus on specific features

The rule of thumb is not to reference a person in the cover letter or your references if there is any doubt in your mind as to their reputation with all stakeholder groups in the school community.

or programs of the district that this person called to your attention and you must be sure that this person's reputation will add to your appeal and not detract. We have seen more than a few candidates not called in because the person they referenced was not a high performing employee of the district or was a very negative force in the school culture and there was no interest in bringing on someone with similar qualities. Sometimes even the old family friend who you think is the nicest guy in the world can be a different person at work. The rule of thumb is not to reference a person in the cover letter or your references if there is any doubt in your mind as to their reputation with all stakeholder groups in the school community.

Chapter

5

Researching the School and District Before the Interview

Schools are full of pride and tradition. We have seen more than one interviewing committee turned off by a teaching candidate who did not do their homework on the school or district they were seeking to work for. Remember, the people interviewing you want to see a candidate who really wants to be a part of their school, their faculty, and their community. We know that candidates who do not complete their research before the interview significantly reduce their chance to win the position. Principals, teachers and members of the interview committees don't expect you to know everything about the school, but they do expect that you cared and showed enough respect to do the research that you could.

...candidates who do not complete their research before the interview significantly reduce their chance to win the position.

Good news! We have some recommendations that will help you prepare before the interview and subsequently help you during your interview:

- Know the school district's basic demographic data. For example, the number of schools, students, teachers, teacher/pupil ratio, average class size, geographic boundaries, socioeconomics, grade levels served, etcetera. In essence, we recommend that you have a feel for the district. Our point is: A school district with 800 students is much different than a district with 8000. You want to make sure you are applying to a district that is a good fit for you personally.

- Read the district's mission and vision statements. If they are simple enough, memorize them. Although we have seen it, the odds are unlikely they will ask you this, but you never know when they will come in handy in a response or written task. If they are longer statements, just put the essence or a few key words to memory.

- Read the school's goals and any plans that they have for the future. Many districts and schools have long-range plans on their websites. These can provide valuable information about leadership, what the district values, and where their priorities are for the future.

- Know the district's professional development initiatives. Be sure to research them thoroughly and be able to speak to them intelligently.

- This can be difficult to do, but try to know the principal by sight and (if possible) others who will be a part of the interview team. This way you can use the principal's name immediately and avoid introductions. School websites often provide pictures off administration, faculty and board of education members that will assist with getting to know the key players by sight before you come before the committee.

- Gather as much information about the department or grade level related to what you teach. Know what their initiatives and special units they are working on so you can applaud the things that they are doing. More importantly, this will protect you from a misstep during the interview such as criticizing something they believe in. The essential point is that armed with this information you will be able to highlight your strengths and show how you would be a good fit for the grade level team or department.

- Investigate the district in the local newspapers, community newsletters, and read the superintendent's messages on the web. It is valuable to know what the district is dealing with right now. For example, budget constraints, implementation of new programs, staff reductions, failure to meet learning standards, building construction, accolades etc. This information can be very valuable to you during the interview. Here's a quick example. Let's say you did your research and found that the high school was transitioning to a block schedule. You then could most assuredly predict that there would be a question on your feelings about teaching in the block. Assuming you were generally in agreement with this approach, you could plan on stating how much you would like the opportunity to teach in the block providing evidence to the committee that your teaching beliefs match the direction the school is headed. Knowing this information gives you an edge because you are able to predict questions and prepare for them beforehand.

- Investigate the district's mentoring program and know generally what it entails. All districts these days have mentoring programs. Many states mandate that they have them. Be prepared to speak to how a mentoring relationship would benefit you as a professional striving to get better and to be the best that you can be.

- Look at the district data available on your state education department's website. This will give you a good grasp of the general academic profile of the district, the subject area and the grade level that you are applying for.

- Research the school's extracurricular and athletic programs and have a feel for what is offered. Principals are always interested in teachers who are willing to involve themselves outside the classroom. This research will give you an idea of the extracurricular and athletic programs you may be interested in. Remember, there is only one head football coach or advisor to the art club so be open to other opportunities to interact with students.

- Finally, take a drive through the district and acquaint yourself with the socioeconomic environment, the upkeep of the schools and grounds, etcetera. This drive will also serve a dual purpose as it will ensure that you know how to get to the exact building and entry for the interview so you are sure to arrive on time.

Here is a Pre-Interview Research Checklist. It lists all the steps to be taken in preparation for the interview. Use this as an organizational tool each time you have an interview to make sure you have done a thorough job researching the school and district.

Fig. 5.1 Pre-Interview Checklist: Researching the School & District

❑ I know the school's/district's basic demographic data (i.e. number of schools, students, teachers, teacher/pupil ratio, average class size, geographic boundaries, grade levels served, etc.). In essence, I have a feel for the district and see it as a good fit for me.

❑ I have read the district/school's mission statement/vision statement and would be able to reference them in the interview.

❑ I have read the district/school's goals and any plans that they have for the future. Many districts and schools have long-range plans on their websites. These can provide valuable information about leadership, what the district values, and where their priorities are for the future.

❑ I know the school's/district's professional development initiatives. Regardless of what they are i.e. Robert Marzano's *What Works in Schools*, Silver and Strong's *The Thoughtful Teacher*, etc.. I have researched them thoroughly and am able to speak to them intelligently.

❑ I will know the principal by sight and others (if possible) who will be a part of the interview team or process. I have looked them up on the school or district website.

❑ I looked at the content area/grade level related to what I teach. I know special units they are working on and what the department initiatives are so I can applaud the things that they are doing to try to help kids and am able to highlight my strengths to show how I would be a good fit as a colleague.

❑ I know what the teacher/administrative leadership (i.e School Improvement Team or Building Planning committees) are implementing. I believe in what they are doing. I have spent time thinking about my own personal skills, how I could be beneficial to their goals and how I could help.

❑ I have read the hot topics in the local newspapers, the community newsletters, and the superintendent's messages regarding the district and community on the web. I have an understanding of what the district is dealing with right now i.e. budget constraints, new initiatives, staff reductions, not meeting learning standards, building construction, etc.

❑ I have investigated the district's mentoring program and know exactly what it entails. I am prepared to speak to it based on how it would benefit me as a professional striving to grow.

❑ I have investigated the district's curriculum maps. I have looked at the curriculum maps in the department/grade level and feel comfortable talking about them, their direction, and philosophy in my answers to potential interview questions.

❑ I have a feel for the district's data available on the state's website and on the district's website. I feel I have a good grasp of the "bare bones" of the district and the department/grade level that I am applying for. I understand how they performed last year and beyond and can reasonably predict their goals for the coming school year.

❑ I have found and am cognizant of the Board of Education Goals for this year.

❑ I have researched the district's K-12 student achievement results in ELA and Math. (Even if you are not in these content areas we still recommend that you research this information as they drive decision-making regarding professional development and impact all content areas in meaningful ways.)

❑ I have researched the district/school's extra-curricular and athletic programs and have a feel for what is offered and their quality. I have spent some time thinking about what areas would be of interest to me and how I could get involved in the school district.

❑ I have researched the district/school's technological initiatives. I know what technology is available to faculty and expectations for its use.

❑ I have driven through the district and acquainted myself with the socio-economic environment, the upkeep of the schools and grounds, etc.

❑ I know what building my interview will be held in. I know how to get there and the correct entry to use.

Recommended Interview Attire and Personal Appearance

What you wear to the interview and your personal appearance will make a big difference. From the moment you walk in the door, both send clear messages to the individuals on the interview team. Dressing appropriately is a compliment to the person you meet. If in doubt, our recommendation is to err on the side of dressing one step above what you may feel is required. Your attire should speak well of you and the impression you are trying to make, but not take center stage. If you walk out of an interview and are remembered for your interview attire, you made an error in judgment.

Some of this may seem obvious, but trust us, it is worth reviewing. We have seen many mistakes in interviews and at teacher recruitment days that could have been avoided. We understand that times change, fashion changes, and our culture changes. However, our mission is to help you get the teaching position that you desire. Sometimes landing that job may mean altering your own personal styles and maybe even conforming to show that you have the flexibility and judgment to meet the district's needs as a professional.

We understand that times change, fashion changes, and our culture changes. However, our mission is to help you get the teaching position that you desire. Sometimes landing that job may mean altering your own personal styles and maybe even conforming to show that you have the flexibility and judgment to meet the district's needs as a professional.

It is important to understand that the principals, teachers, and parents who are on the interview teams are for the most part, older than you. When they grew up it was very rare, we might even say eccentric, for people to have tattoos. And no one had piercings in the way that people do today. Education in this regard is very conservative. We strongly recommend that you save these types of items and personal styles for the weekend and for after the interview. Our advice, having collectively done hundreds of interviews with hiring committees is to cover up your tattoos, remove your piercings, and men- take out the earrings.

There are no doubt exceptions. Certain settings and committees would not hold earrings, tattoos, extreme hairs styles etc. against you. In some settings, it might even play to your advantage to reflect a more progressive personal style. However, we advise that you be extremely confident of your audience before you decide to abandon a conservative approach to dress and style. And you should know that no matter how open-minded or 'fashion forward' a school community is about these issues, no one is looking to hire someone who is not cleanly and well put together.

Below, we've listed some more specific recommendations:

Interview Attire Guidelines for Men:
Suit: No one on the interview team expects you to be able to afford an Armani suit. But, we suggest that you buy one or two good quality conservative suits. A two-piece matched suit is always the best and the safest choice. Stick with conservative colors for example, navy, charcoal, and dark

gray and be sure to choose a fabric that can be worn year round. Wool, wool blends, or very high quality blends with natural fiber, are the way to go.

Ties: Select a good quality conservative tie that goes subtly with the suit and shirt. Avoid fashion extremes like character ties, fluorescent colors, etc.

Facial hair: Facial hair should be well-groomed, neat, and clean.

Shirts: Long-sleeved shirts, even in summer. We recommend that you stick with white or a solid light blue.

Belt: Black, brown, or cordovan leather that match your shoes.

Socks: Dark socks, long enough so that no skin is visible when you sit down.

Shoes: Leather business shoes: black, brown, or cordovan. A nice shiny pair of good shoes makes the outfit. Be sure your shoes are shined before the interview.

Jewelry: Wear a conservative watch. If you choose to wear other jewelry, be conservative.

Interview Attire Guidelines for Women:
Cosmetics: Keep makeup conservative. A little is usually better than none for a polished look. Nails should be clean and well groomed. Avoid extreme nail length and color as they can be distracting to interviewers.

Suit: Wear a two-piece matched business suit. Tailored pants and skirts are appropriate for women. Pants should be creased and tailored, not tight or flowing.

Skirt lengths: Your skirt should cover your thighs when you are sitting at the interview table. A skirt that ends at the knee when you are standing looks professional. High slits in skirts are not appropriate. On a calf length skirt, a slit to the knee to facilitate walking and climbing stairs is recommended.

Shirt/Sweaters: Underneath the suit jacket, wear a tailored blouse in a color or small print that coordinates nicely with your suit. A fine gauge, good quality knit shell is also appropriate underneath your suit jacket.

Color/Fabric: Navy, dark gray, brown and black are safe. Again, avoid the fashion extremes. Choose a solid or very subtle weave pattern. Wool, wool blends, and high quality blends and synthetics are appropriate for women's suits.

Jewelry/Accessories: We recommend simple and basic jewelry i.e. one earring in each ear, necklace, and watch.

Shoes: Should be leather, fabric or micro fiber. Regardless of what is in style, avoid extremes. Polished and closed toe shoes, basic dark pumps with medium or low heels, no high heels or platform shoes. Make certain you can walk comfortably in your shoes.

Leg Wear: Should be plainly styled (no patterns), sheer (not opaque), and in neutral colors complementing your suit. Avoid high contrast between your suit and leg wear.

Purse or Bag: Do your best to leave your purse at home or safely secured in your car. You will have a portfolio and other things to carry. We believe it is important to enter the room fully able to immediately shake hands and engage each one of the interviewers. You can't do this fumbling with a purse, briefcase, portfolio and resumes all at once.

Chapter

7

Stages of the Interview Process

To understand how to succeed at a teaching interview, you need to be fully aware of the process that will unfold. Despite what your college career office may tell you, you are not going to walk into a school and sit down to chat with the principal over a cup of coffee. Those days are long gone.

The investment that schools are making in their new hires is under escalating scrutiny. By our estimates, the average American public school district will invest somewhere around three and half million dollars in salary, benefits and other expenses in a teacher who serves in that district for thirty years. The process to

...schools have become increasingly specialized in their processes for hiring to improve the odds they will 'get it right.' They have departed from typical approaches used in other professions.

remove an ineffective teacher can be cumbersome, costly or impossible depending upon the state or district. Consequently, schools have become increasingly specialized in their processes for hiring to improve the odds that they will 'get it right.' They have departed from typical approaches used in other professions.

Understanding the stages used in education will go a long way in decreasing your anxiety on interview day. Over the past several years, we have carefully studied and identified the stages we believe are most prevalent among schools in order to maximize the likelihood that you are going to know exactly what is going to take place as you interview for a position. There are, without a doubt, variations on how schools will implement these stages. In addition, new techniques for reviewing teacher

Understanding the stages that you will be faced with as a part of the specialized hiring approaches in education will go a long way in decreasing your anxiety on interview day.

candidates are constantly evolving to keep pace with contemporary instructional methods and professional expectations. Here are the stages you can typically expect to be a part of today's teacher interview process:

Stage 1: The Search

The search for a teacher begins when schools go through dozens of applications. This initial screening is usually done by an assistant principal, principal, or department chair. Some schools have clear criteria, rubrics or score sheets when screening applications. However, from our experience and research, in most districts this is a very cursory and subjective process. This is why we encourage you to get to know the principal, department chair, and classroom teachers as a substitute or teacher assistant. If they are happy with your performance and like you, your resume will be in the finalist pile before they even begin this initial search. GPA is always scrutinized at this stage, so again, take your studies seriously.

After the initial scrutiny, schools next look for fit in terms of the needs of the department and school. The coursework you completed as a part of your graduate and/or undergraduate degrees, your certifications, as well as the courses you are most suited to teach may all play a role in whether you get called in for an interview. Much depends upon where they need to cover areas where they lack specialists or shore up liabilities. As an elementary educator, your content area strength will come into play as schools usually want grade level teachers with different content specialties.

If your CV is plucked from the pile, you may receive a screening call to see how you stack up against the district's initial rubric or to clarify details of your experience, education or certification.

▌▌▌ Insider Edge Doc ▶

Below is an actual example of a form used to conduct initial screenings of candidate resumes. The appendix to this book contains several more examples of initial screening documents from schools around the country and reference check forms. You will quickly notice the attributes they are looking for as well as questions you should be prepared to respond to.

Figure 7.1 Cover Letter & Resume Initial Screening Document
ABC School District
Teacher Candidate Cover Letter & Resume Review

Candidate's Name: _____ Position: _____

GPA Undergraduate:	GPA Undergraduate Major:	GPA Graduate:

Quality of Pedagogical Coursework
Assessment (Circle One & Notes?): Cool 1 2 3 4 5 Warm

Quality of Content Related Coursework
Assessment (Circle One & Notes?): Cool 1 2 3 4 5 Warm

Document is Professional in Appearance/Format?
Assessment (Circle One & Notes?): Cool 1 2 3 4 5 Warm

Past Teaching Experiences
Assessment (Circle One & Notes?): Cool 1 2 3 4 5 Warm

Past Experiences Supervising Student Extra Curricular Activities
Assessment (Circle One & Notes?): Cool 1 2 3 4 5 Warm

Commitment to Professional Development
Assessment (Circle One & Notes?): Cool 1 2 3 4 5 Warm

Overall assessment of candidate? Cool 1 2 3 4 5 **Warm**
Granted interview? YES NO RESERVE LIST Screener Initials:

Do not get down on yourself or angry if you fail to get past stage one, even if this occurs multiple times. You never know what types of special content needs the school had and what types of arguments may have taken place behind closed doors. You may very well have been the strongest candidate, but did not a match for the needs of the moment.

Stage 2: Introductory Stage

If you pass stage one, you will receive an invitation to interview. You will arrive at the interview site and someone will be designated, usually a secretary, to greet you, offer you a seat, ask you to wait until the interview team is ready to see you.

▌▌▌ Insider Edge Note

It may seem like commonsense, but this is an important reminder be nice to everyone associated with an interview. The support-staff you meet in the offices are important to the process. Their opinions are informally solicited, or given even when not solicited, and they do matter. A simple comment by a secretary to the building principal can, and often does, make a difference.

It is almost always that the building principal will come out next to greet you and then lead you to the room where the interview committee is conducting the interviews. You have a choice here. Immediately sit in the hot seat or proceed to shake all interviewers' hands. Our recommendation is that you establish a connection right away. Introduce yourself to every member of the committee and shake each one of their hands. Be sure the handshake is firm, but not crushing, and look them in the eyes while shaking.

You should be aware that these committees are not just comprised of teachers and administrators. Typically they will include parent representatives and, at the secondary level, student representatives. Some districts will purposely choose not to identify the roles of the committee members in their community or to introduce them individually. Do not be shaken by this approach. This is often done for the sake of time or to keep the committee members from getting distracted by personal contacts or pleasantries.

Be sure that you do not talk down to the student representatives. They have been selected by the school as leaders and are ahead of their peers on the maturity curve. They will be conducting themselves as adults and it will be awkward if you treat them any differently from the rest of the committee. Take their questions seriously because their voice will be important in candidate selection.

Insider Edge Note

> When you are shaking each committee member's hand, try your best to remember their name. As soon as you sit down, quickly jot down the names of the people around the table. In this way, you then will be able to use their names when answering their questions. There is a very powerful aspect of using a person's name in the answer to their question. Adopting and practicing this technique has value, but we only recommend this for those individuals who are confident enough and are able to use it without coming off as phony or disingenuous. We do not recommend its use if we see a candidate who is nervous or potentially overwhelmed by the interview experience. It is not necessary so do not feel compelled to try to incorporate it into your interview. However, when done well it can be a very effective tool.

From here, the lead interviewer (again, usually the building principal) will establish rapport and try to create a relaxed, though professional, atmosphere. Remember, this is where the interviewers get their very important first impression of you. Smile. Be enthusiastic. Be excited about the opportunity. Be yourself.

The principal will usually say a few opening words, perhaps talk about the position available, perhaps the time frame for hiring, perhaps the next steps in the process, perhaps what they are looking for in the successful candidate. But eventually the introductory stage of the interview will come to an end when the questioning begins.

Look for an opening during the introductory stage to mention that you have brought your portfolio and ask if the committee would like to send it around the table. Our recommendation is to leave your portfolio behind with the committee and to pick it up later. This gives the interview team more time to peruse your work. Bringing a duplicate, digital version, or web address with your online portfolio to leave with committee members is also a good idea, but be sure they get a good look at the original version of your portfolio and artifacts at some point. Copies often do not do justice to your original and there is no guarantee they are going to take the time to get to a computer and view your digital/online portfolio before they make a decision.

Stage 3: Who Are You?- A Review of Your Background

The vast majority of the time this takes the form of, "Well Sara, why don't you begin by telling us a little about yourself both personally and professionally." "What," "why," "where," and "when" types of questions may follow this. We'll talk a little more about how to tackle this question when we get down to types of interview questions and strategies in chapter eight.

Stage 4: Around the Horn with Questions

Typically, each interviewer will be equipped with a question or two. These questions will have some sort of rating scale attached to them such as a simple Likert Scale (1-5). The interview team may have discussed beforehand what kinds of responses they are looking for and have, in essence, created a verbal rubric. Other times, there is a written rubric attached to the question. Each committee member will have a question(s) assigned to them and they will go around the table taking turns asking the interviewee questions until all have been asked.

The next two pages provide an example of a rubric used by a school stakeholder committee to assess candidate responses during interviews. The appendix to this book contains several more examples of these rubrics used by schools across the country. Study them and you'll get a feel for how committees go about grading your responses to 'around the horn' questioning.

Figure 7.2 Portion of an Interview Committee Around the Horn Rubric

Lincoln CSD- Elementary Teacher Interview Rubric		
Date: Candidate:		
Committee Member:		
1. *Welcome…. Begin by telling us a little about yourself, your experience and background.*		
Notes…..		
2. *Parent communications are a very important component of classroom success. Please share what forms of communication you have (or will) implement in your classroom.*		
3	**2**	**1**
• Discusses multiple forms such as notes, calls, newsletters, journal/assignment notebooks, etc. • Emphasizes both positive and negative nature of communication. • Indicates a timely response to a parent's initiation of a concern. • Display various samples within their portfolio as evidence of parent communication.	• Discusses minimal forms of avenues to communicate to parents. • Emphasizes either positive or negative nature of communication. • Indicates a response to a parent's initiation of a concern. • Little evidence of parent communication in samples/portfolio.	• Discusses only planned parent/teacher conferences. • Briefly touches, if at all, on positive or negative nature of communication • May or may not indicate a response to a parent's concern. • Weak evidence of parent communication in samples/portfolio.
Notes…..		
3. *You have a child in your classroom who constantly speaks out, does not remain seated, and never does any homework. You have already spoken to the parents and nothing has changed. What will you do now?*		
3	**2**	**1**
• Identifies a behavior management plan with details utilizing other building personnel. • May include a description of specific behavioral strategies such as individual behavior plans and exhibit an understanding of discipline theories.	• Identifies a behavior management plan that is general and does not include specific details for implementation.	• No mention of a behavior plan but indicates that they would send student to administrator.

Notes…..

4. *You are certified to teach in K-6 grades, choose a specific grade level and describe your literacy program that you believe will meet the needs of all of your learners.*

3	2	1
• Discusses specific ELA Standards (links literacy with Reading, Writing, Speaking and Listening). • Describes components of a balanced literacy program, describes diagnostic assessments, and interdisciplinary strategies.	• Discusses general ELA Standards (vaguely relates literacy with Reading, Writing, Speaking and Listening). • Mentions parts of a literacy program. • May only name specific programs without evidence of understanding.	• Discussion of program is weak and limited • May use literal interpretation of ELA Standards or literacy programs.

Notes…..

5. *You have just administered a practice math test to your ____ graders (which aligns with the Grade 4 Math). Several of your students have scored well below a passing score. What are you going to do now?*

3	2	1
• Discusses varied instructional strategies such as Differentiated Instruction, flexible grouping, learning centers, learning styles, multiple intelligences, etc. • Identifies potential strategies to address upper end as well as lower end students. • Provides specific details. • May mention data analysis.	• Merely mentions a few instructional strategies such as Differentiated Instruction, flexible grouping, learning centers, learning styles, multiple intelligences, etc. • May mention a specific program.	• Describes limited strategies that may include passing on to a resource or remedial teacher.

Notes…..

Stage 5: Your Questions for the Committee

In this stage, the vast majority of the time, the principal will announce that the questions from the committee are complete and then ask if there are any questions that the candidate has for them. The options and our advice on this are a part of chapter nine. Regardless of what you decide, try to end on a high note. Do not forget to maintain your enthusiasm, and smile, smile, smile.

Stage 6: The Teaching Demonstration

In this stage, three to four candidates will be offered an opportunity to come in and do a teaching demonstration. This stage can take place at either the start or end of the interview process or as a follow-up to the initial interview. We will get into some real specifics on the teaching demonstration in chapter eleven of this book.

Stage 7: The Written Task

In this part of the interview process, you will be asked to work alone to complete a task. This may occur before or after your interview with the stakeholder committee. The length of these tasks vary from about fifteen minutes to forty-five. Sometimes you will be asked to complete the task by hand. Increasingly, schools are seating candidates at computer to complete their written task. Not only do they get to assess your writing, content, organizational, and pedagogical skills, they get the bonus of taking a look at how well you manage technology.

Written task topics can vary widely. Sometimes they will be flat out measures of your content knowledge. For example, math teachers might be given a part of an actual AP examination to complete or social studies teachers may be asked to complete a document based question from a state assessment. They might ask you to reflect upon your teaching demonstration or even to write a letter to parents of your new students if you were to be given the position. Some schools will provide you with a topic and ask you to write a lesson plan. We have heard of situations where candidates were asked to write a lesson plan and then deliver it to the committee as their teaching demonstration. Having candidates review video of another teacher's classroom and provide analysis is also becoming popular.

███ **Insider Edge Note**

This is the most popular written task we have come across after sampling from hundreds of schools from across the country:

"You have just finished your teaching demonstration. Upon reflection, what worked, what didn't work, and what would you have changed if you had the opportunity to teach this lesson again?"

This task gives the principal and the committee immediate feedback on whether the teacher was able to effectively reflect on the lesson just presented, diagnose areas for growth and determine next steps if this were their real classroom. Principals often want to see if the candidate caught the same successes and liabilities that the committee caught.

The ability to reflect and self-assess is a valued commodity for contemporary educators. Schools do not want to invest in teachers who feel they have nothing to learn once in the classroom or lack the ability to diagnose when their efforts are not successful.

Regardless of the format of the written task, we encourage you to do the following:

- Take three minutes to plan out your response on scrap paper so it follows a logical progression
- Be sure your response is professionally formatted
- Check for grammatical and spelling errors. Use the built in tools for this if using a computer, but make sure you reread your final product.
- If you are asked to tackle a pedagogical issue, inject reference to research and contemporary teaching and learning practices.
- Take a copy of your writing with you (if permitted) so that even if you do not get this job you can review it to improve your performance in future written-tasks.

▌▌▌ Insider Edge Doc ➤

The appendix to this book contains many more examples of written tasks specific to each content area. Head to the back of the book and see what committees are asking people from your certification area to write about!

Stage 8: The Final Interview

In this stage, usually you are one of two finalists. It is likely you will be interviewed by the Superintendent or the Assistant Superintendent of Personnel. During this interview, you will encounter questions similar to the first interview. Remember, they need to get to know you just as well as the committee you met with, so your training and preparation for the committee interview should apply here as well.

▌▌▌ Insider Edge Note ➤

We advise that you do not talk about money issues at this stage, unless asked. This can be a real turnoff to school administrators who may see you as more focused on the highest possible compensation rather than an intrinsic passion for educating young people. This could cost you the job.

If you do get a call offering you the position, this would be the time to discuss pay and benefits. Even now, you need to do it carefully, particularly if this is a position you really want and need. Many schools have contracts with their teachers associations that really box-in the conversation when it comes to benefits and salary, so there may not be much negotiation to take place at all. This is particularly true if you are dealing with a traditional public school or school district. If you are applying to a private or charter school, there may be some flexibility here.

If you have no teaching experience, we recommend that you do not try to haggle and get steps at all. The result may be that you haggle yourself out of a job. But if you have legitimate teaching experience in another district or school, the correct time to seek compensation for that service is when you are offered the job. Once you sign your contract, that opportunity will almost always be lost forever. Superintendents and heads of school do have flexibility here if you have previous experience, but they are weighing hiring you over the other candidate, which is an unknown variable to you. The ugly reality of business and life is that hiring you at a higher cost might be less desirable than hiring the other candidate at a lesser cost, so be careful.

The best way to initiate this conversation is to say, "Can you tell me about your district's salary and benefit scale and how I would fit into that?" Or "Is there someone available to review how I would fit into your district's salary and benefits package when I come in to complete paperwork?"

Interview Questions:
The EDU Edge 'Umbrella Approach'

We believe that interviewing is similar to other performances you might prepare for such as a speech, a part in a musical, or an athletic event. The skills that are needed can be developed. The event itself can be simulated and practiced ahead of time with the right information. We also believe that your confidence grows through the belief that you are well prepared and know what to expect. That preparation must begin well in advance of the actual interview.

The EDU Edge has gathered questions asked by interview teams all over the country. After studying literally thousands of questions, we have been able to identify patterns and commonalities that have allowed us to divide them into twelve domains. Each of these domains is addressed by one 'umbrella' question that we feel covers the domain and, if well prepared, can

By mastering responses to these twelve umbrella questions, you will have responses ready for any question an interview committee might throw at you.

be used as a springboard for other answers to similar questions in the domain. By mastering responses to these twelve umbrella questions, you will have responses ready for any question an interview committee might throw at you.

Please understand, these are not the top twelve questions that are asked during teaching interviews. These are the twelve questions that, when practiced, will best prepare you for any question that may be posed to you during the interview. We not only believe, we know from personal experience, that practicing and preparing for these twelve questions will give you 'the edge' in the interview process.

To get started in mastering the twelve domains, take a look at each of the twelve umbrella questions below and write down responses. At first don't be concerned with how long the responses are. Write in complete sentences and make notes along the way on topics that you need to research further. Once you are done with this, now tackle the research. After you have completed your research, go back and adjust the original responses based on this new information.

Condense all the information into a tight response. This response should be what you as an individual would like to say if you could give the perfect interview. This response should be no longer than two and a half minutes when read aloud. Reading aloud is slower and captures more accurately how long the response will be. Read and repeat your answers aloud over and over as if you were studying for a test trying to memorize the answers. Keep your responses to the umbrella questions with you throughout your day and whenever you have an opportunity take them out and practice.

> ### Insider Edge Note
>
> Try to practice giving your responses aloud. Your responses sound much different aloud. This practice is crucial to iron out the kinks. Tape recording yourself, videotaping yourself or having a friend critique you will take this a step further. Another idea is to have a family member or a friend read the questions and then you provide the answers. This too, will go a long way in building your confidence.

Let's take a moment to go through the twelve domains and the umbrella question that helps to illustrate each domain. Once you have prepared and rehearsed your response to each umbrella question, head to the appendix to see how your responses to the umbrella questions can be used interchangeably with dozens of additional questions within the domains. Yes, you will need to make minor modifications to your responses to fit the exact nature of the additional questions within the domain. However, you will find that the heart of the content can remain the same, putting you in the driver's seat when a question is posed to you. It is an incredible edge to be in control of the situation rather than responding to the situation blindly.

> *Knowing what your response will be as soon as the question is asked and getting your point across in a succinct fashion sends a signal to the committee that you will have the same clear direction in leading your classroom.*

Knowing what your response will be as soon as the question is asked and getting your point across in a succinct fashion sends a signal to the committee that you will have the same clear direction in leading your classroom. If you must think up the response as it is being asked, it increases the likelihood that you will hesitate, say something you do not really believe in or wander in your response. Some may think preparing and rehearsing responses ahead of time is superficial. On the contrary, how many people have walked out of an interview saying, "I can't believe I said that! I don't really believe that, I just was searching for something to say." Using our Umbrella Approach and rehearsing allows you to be sure you are able to get across the responses and information you truly believe in.

▌▌▌ Insider Edge Doc

Let's review the twelve domains of questions as well as the Umbrella Questions (UQ) for each domain:

Fig. 8.1 Twelve Interview Question Domains and Umbrella Questions

Domain	Topic	Umbrella Question (UQ)
1	Beginning of Interview: Ice Breakers	Tell us a little about yourself both personally and professionally.
2	About You Personally: Who Are You?	What personal qualities will contribute to your success as a teacher?
3	Professionalism & The Teaching Profession	Who has been your greatest teaching mentor? What characteristics make them a good teacher?
4	Beliefs on Curriculum & Planning	What do you feel are the most important things students learn in your classroom?
5	Beliefs on Instruction	Describe a lesson that worked exceptionally for you. Why do you think it succeeded? Describe a lesson that you consider a failure. Have you been able to diagnose why it was ineffective?
6	Beliefs on Assessment	Define the term assessment and tell us what strategies are most effective for assessing student progress?
7	Classroom Management	What does classroom management mean to you? Please describe the process that you have used in dealing with a student who was disrupting the class.
8	Special Education	Have you worked with special education students in the past? In what capacity? How do you balance the special requirements of students with IEPs with the needs of the remainder of your students?
9	Content Knowledge	Where do your true interests/passions lie within your content area?
10	Knowledge of School or District – School Pride	Why do you want to teach at this school?
11	Parent Communication & Building Relationships	How would you involve parents in their child's academic/discipline problems at school?
12	End of Interview	What questions do you have for us?

Again, these umbrella questions are not the top twelve questions that are asked in teaching interviews. These are the twelve questions that when practiced will best prepare you for any questions that may be thrown at you during a teacher interview.

Let's take a closer look at how this works. Domain six is, 'Beliefs on Assessment.' Assume you have followed our recommendation to write out a thoughtful and researched response to the umbrella question for this domain. You have also rehearsed the response for this Umbrella Question, which is, "Define the term assessment and tell us what strategies are most effective for assessing student progress?"

You are now in the interview and you are asked one of these questions that fall within the same domain. Your practiced response is easily adaptable or used to answer all of these questions:

- What evaluation techniques do you use?
- Describe your grading policy and philosophy.
- How do you measure student performance in your classroom?
- Describe the types of quizzes, tests, projects that you give.
- How should a student's educational achievement and progress be measured?
- How do you know whether your curriculum is appropriately matched to your students' needs?

▌▌▌ Insider Edge Note

Our team at The EDU Edge collected questions from principals and central office administrators from all over the globe and found that committees are asking very similar questions, just in a different way. The questions covered by The EDU Edge 'Umbrella Approach' are not specific to a particular state or region. Depending upon country, they are even useful in international settings where contemporary western instructional philosophies have been adopted. If you practice and prepare for these twelve umbrella questions you will have an arsenal of responses that fit the many permutations of questions that principals or teacher interview committees may throw at you.

So now that you know the twelve domains and twelve umbrella questions it's time to sit down and refine your responses. If you take nothing else from this book, take this: taking the time to do your homework and due diligence on these twelve questions before the interview will give you the edge over other candidates who did not.

Insider Edge Doc

*The appendix to this book contains **over 350 interview questions** that school principals and district human resource officers report asking in interviews! These questions in the appendix are organized into The EDU Edge's 'Twelve Domains.' Use the responses you have developed to the 'Umbrella Questions' and practice the minor adjustments needed to make them work for all questions within the domain.*

End of Interview: Your Questions for the Committee

Most interviewers build in time at the end of the interview for candidates to ask a few questions. It is uncommon when you will not be offered this opportunity. Many candidates will be advised, and will feel pressure, to ask multiple questions to show their level of interest or additional expertise. While there is some opportunity to gain ground at this stage of the interview, we believe there is even greater potential to do damage. Take a look at the two strategies we advise below and you will quickly understand why the conventional thinking just might be dangerous.

Strategy #1: Ask No Questions at All

Yes, asking no questions at all is allowed, and can be a viable strategy! Our rationale is simple. School interview teams screen candidates on very tight schedules. They can become easily frustrated, even if subconsciously, by candidates that are not considerate or dominate their time. From our personal experience it doesn't hurt, and in some cases may help, to not ask any questions at all. When asked, "Do you have any questions?" stating something along the lines of the following is a nice way to bring closure to the interview:

"Of course I have a million questions, but at this point the process and next steps seem clear to me. I would love to be a part of this school and faculty so if I am lucky enough to remain in the process, I will ask them at that time. Again, I just want to thank you all for this wonderful opportunity and for your time."

You can see how this response does not leave you extending the interview unnecessarily. At the same time, it allows you to exit in a professional, confident, and upbeat manner.

▌▌▌ Insider Edge Note

Do not believe the hype! Many internet job search sites and career centers lead you to believe that asking questions at the end of an interview is a must. Please know that you should not feel compelled or pressured to ask questions. We believe that asking questions is not necessary, particularly in earlier screening rounds where committees are dealing with large volumes of candidates. It does not hurt to not ask questions and may help you because it takes the pressure off the principal and interview team who are rushing to get candidates in and out on time. Moreover, it shows that you understand and appreciate the job that they have to accomplish for the day and that you understand your position in the process.

Strategy #2: Ask One, Two or Three *Good* Questions.

Our rationale for this is that you should feel comfortable asking questions if you truly have questions, but make sure that they are "good" questions. "Good" questions are questions that you could not have looked up the answers to by yourself and on your own time. Our strongest recommendation is to ask questions that get the principal and teachers talking about what they are proud of and excited about. Questions that put the interview team in a position to praise themselves, their school, and their students.

> *Our strongest recommendation is to ask questions that get the principal and teachers talking about what they are proud of and excited about.*

Examples of "Good" Questions are:

- This seems like a great school district. What are you most proud of about your school?
- This school seems to have a nice learning atmosphere. What would faculty, students, and parents say are the strengths of your school that lead to this?
- I really want to help this school in any way that I am able. What priorities would you have for me as a new faculty member?
- Every school is special in some way. How is this school special?
- What unique strengths and needs does this school have that distinguish it from others in the area?

A special plea: your grandma was correct, there are no dumb questions. However, we believe that asking certain questions at the end of the interview is dumb. We recommend in the strongest terms that you do not ask questions that are clearly answered on the employer's web site, in district literature, or on any other websites such as the state's department of education website. Here are just a few examples of questions you could ask that are going to reflect negatively on you.

Your grandma was correct, there are no dumb questions. However, we believe that asking certain questions at the end of the interview is dumb.

They are all things you should be curious about, but there are many sources besides the hiring committee that can provide you with this information before you walk into that room:

- What are the demographics of the school/district?
- What's the average class size?
- What is the teacher/student ratio in your district?
- What is your school building like?
- What sports teams or extracurricular clubs does your school have?
- Do you have a mentoring program?
- In what ways do you encourage teachers to engage in professional development?

Asking these types of questions quickly reveals that you did not properly prepare for the interview or are inconsiderate of the committee's time. It will speak negative volumes when it comes to your initiative, attention to detail, and ultimately your candidacy. The employer will always be courteous and professional when answering these questions, but behind the scenes they are likely thinking and feeling that you are unprepared and putting them behind schedule.

The moral of the story is, if you have questions, ask them. But, be sure that they are good questions and that you are asking them in a sincere way as opposed to asking them because you feel they are a required part of the interview. There is no shame in not picking up points on this part of the interview where there is greater risk than rewards available.

Insider Edge Note

Even at this stage, we recommend that you never ask about salary and benefits until they are brought up to you. Usually this opportunity is not going to come until you are offered a position and even then, must be handled carefully as discussed in Chapter 7 about the stages of the interview process. Asking about pay, salary, even working conditions such as hours and number of duties shows improper etiquette similar to asking how much someone earns per year. Almost all interview teams are charged with screening candidates and then recommending one to three candidates to the personnel department or to the superintendent of schools. These teams or principals are put in place to screen and pick the best candidates for their schools but almost never have the authority to negotiate or discuss salary and benefits. So don't ask them. The time will come to get this information and for you to try to negotiate the best deal you can. Trust us, you will not start teaching without having these questions explained to you. Wait for the appropriate administrator to bring it up or until you are offered the position. Then use the language we suggest in Chapter 7 to ask these questions so that you do not offend.

After the Interview:
The 'Thank You' Note

We recommend following your mother's age old, but wise advice: "Whenever someone does something nice for you, send them a thank you note." Think about it. You've just finished the interview. The principal and interview team gave you an opportunity to sell yourself as the right teacher for their students. They provided you a shot at a stable career, a good salary, nice medical benefits and entry into one of the best retirement systems in the world. They are considering trusting you to be the one to educate the young people of their community. You have thanked them on the way out the door, but so will every other candidate. You owe them a special thank you. Always write a thank you note!

You need every possible edge over the other candidates and writing a thank you note can contribute to that edge

The thank you note should not be neglected in today's tight and competitive job market. You need every possible edge over the other candidates and writing a thank you note can contribute to that edge. The next morning as the principal is going through their morning mail, there is your note, thanking her for the privilege to interview for the position at their fine school. Trust us, it makes a difference. Even if the district has no opening for you now, there is always a chance something will come available later or at another building and you want to be remembered favorably. We can tell you that as a part of our hiring experience alone, we have had multiple situations where our committees did not hire a competitive candidate for whatever reason, but the memory of the candidate was so positive that it led them to be hired when we referred them to another principal with an opening or hired them ourselves for another opening that became available soon after.

Insider Edge Note

Think that a thank you note won't be noticed? Despite what you may assume, it is the rare candidate that sends a thank you note. Even though moms for generations have taught their children this skill and tried to engrain into them that it is the right thing to do, principals surveyed around the country by The EDU Edge find that very, very few teaching candidates actually make the effort to complete this final step.

We recommend that you get a thank you note in the principal's hands as soon as possible, but at least within twenty-four hours. From our experience, principals and interview committees usually select the candidate for the job or to go on to the next round right after they interview the last candidate for the day. Some may decide to convene again the next day after reflecting upon candidates, but it is rare that this is going to occur because it is difficult to get all of the stakeholders on the committee together for more than one day in a row. However, this should not deter you from sending the thank you note. For a number of reasons your note can still make an impact:

- Sometimes the committee is on the fence between candidates and will need to use reference checks as the tie breaker. These usually take time to complete and the reference check could turn up something on another candidate that puts you back in the game even if you were not originally selected.

- Other candidates ahead of you may pull out of the process or land another job.
- If you are moving on to an additional round, it may help you in a number of ways such as bolstering the principal's recommendation for you to the superintendent.

The bottom line is that you never know what twists and turns the process is going to take, so even though the committee may make their decision before it is possible for them to read your thank you note, be sure you still follow through and get that thank you note in the hands of the principal as soon as humanly possible.

A few notes about the thank you note itself:

- The thank you should be short and to the point but sincere. Do not spend hours on this as the most important thing is likely that you are writing one and other candidates are probably not.
- Be sure that you are using accurate names/roles.
- Express your appreciation and enthusiasm. Be crystal clear that you genuinely appreciated the opportunity to interview with them. Be enthusiastic about the school and the specific position for which you interviewed.
- There are many opinions about the presentation style of thank you letters. We are divided about this as well. We do recommend that you consider typing the thank you note in a standard business-style format, triple checking for typos and grammatical errors. However, we also have seen beautifully handwritten cards on personal stationary that were very sharp as well. If you don't have this type of personal stationary or have disastrous handwriting, go with the typed note.
- Email is an option if you have no other way to get a hand or typewritten note to the administrator, but we do not recommend you use it as a first option. The personal note shows a certain level of care and interest that the convenience of an email fails to convey.

Insider Edge Note

Here is an easy way to get a personalized thank you note to the principal as soon as possible. Before you head to the interview, preaddress and stamp an envelope to the school. Bring along a sharp looking card or piece of stationary to enclose as well. When you complete your interview, head to the nearest library or coffee house and handwrite a personalized thank you note to the committee. Drop it to the nearest post office and the principal should have it the next day. Your thank you note will likely be the first to make an impression and it will be one less thing you have to worry about later that evening!

The Teaching Demonstration: What Happens Behind the Scenes

While the practice of having teaching candidates do a demonstration lesson is still relatively new in some districts or schools, it is also important to note that it also varies quite a bit from school to school. We will describe the sequence of events that is generally reflective of what happens in school districts across the country according to our research, but be prepared for some variation.

In most schools, the first round interview process reduces the number of remaining candidates to three or four applicants. Next, the school schedules teaching demonstrations for each of the remaining candidates. There are two different types of audiences you will generally encounter for these demonstrations: with an actual class of students or with the interview committee pretending they are students.[2] If the lesson will be conducted with an actual class of students, the content department then provides the principal with a date convenient for a teaching demonstration (usually 2-4 days after traditional interview process) and content objectives candidates should deliver.

---

[2] Some school district contracts exclude the use of students during the interview process in this fashion.

Next, applicants are contacted with the time of the demonstration lesson, the lesson topic, and other information (a list of available technology, materials, etc. that are available to use during their lesson). If possible, the school will try to have all teachers teach the same topic and in a similar classroom; for example all grade nine English language arts classes. This is done to provide for a fair and equitable evaluation as well as consistent comparisons between the various candidate demonstrations.

When you arrive in the office on the day of teaching demonstration, someone from the interview committee will greet you while another goes to the classroom and explains the format to actual students or committee members functioning as students. From our experience, the things that are stressed with students in the classroom before your arrival are:

- The committee values their opinion and that it is important for them to have a voice.
- Students are also asked to be courteous and respectful. The goal is not to see how the teacher handles discipline problems, but instead how the teacher carries out instruction and if they are successful in teaching the topic.

When the students are all ready to go, someone from the interview committee will walk you up to the classroom. In cases where actual students are used, the interview committee will sit in the back of the classroom. Each member will take notes on the successes and what the teacher could have done better during the lesson.

When the teaching demonstration ends, the committee will return to the office to process the results with the exception of the one committee member who is responsible for talking to students and getting their feedback. Each member will rate the demonstration and is given a few minutes to explain why they rated in the way that they did. Usually the committee will recommend two candidates to the superintendent. In larger school districts, the principal and/or content area director may handle this final interview.

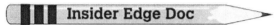 **Insider Edge Doc**

Here is an example of a document used to rate a teaching demonstration (additional rating forms for teaching demonstrations can be found in the appendix):

Fig. 11.1- Teaching Demonstration Rating Document

JEFFERSON CENTRAL SCHOOL DISTRICT
30 Minute Teaching Demonstration
Rating Form

Name: _____ **Grade:** _____ **Size of group:** _____ **Date:** _____

_____ 1. **Preparation and Organization:** (Teacher appears to be well prepared and materials are organized and prepared in advance. The LP contains common core standards, essential question(s), learning goal(s).

_____ 2. **Professionalism:** (Teacher uses valuing responses with the children, even if they make an error; no sarcasm, shows ease and rapport, and is professionally attired.)

_____ 3. **Presentation during teaching:** (Teacher is enthusiastic and articulate, circulates throughout the room, demonstrates knowledge of literacy instructional strategies.)

_____ 4. **Purpose of Lesson Clear:** (Children understand why they are learning what they are learning, learning goals are clear; there is an anticipatory set or hook to the lesson.)

_____ 5. **Authentic Practice:** (Children are learning through purposeful activities/strategies. Teacher uses best practices, wait time, checks for understanding, and monitors and adjusts instruction)

_____ 6. **Active Engagement:** (Children are <u>actively involved</u> in large group, small group, or individual instruction.

_____ 7. **Modeled important elements:** (Reading or writing strategy, etc.)

_____ 8. **Instructional transitions of the lesson:** (Activities relate to the essential question(s) or learning goal(s). There are clear directions.)

_____ 9. **Classroom management:** (Teacher demonstrates class control without punitive measures, uses positive feedback and reinforcement.)

_____ 10. **Provides a Closure:** (Children understand <u>why</u> they learned what they learned or how the learning might be generalized to different material.)

Circle One For Overall Evaluation

1	2	3	4
Does not meet criteria	**Needs improvement**	**Proficient**	**Distinguished (exceeds expectations)**

Comments:

The 'Do's' of the Teaching Demonstration:

- 👍 Smile.
- 👍 Provide committee members with a printed copy of your lesson plan; preferably before the demonstration begins so they will have context for the lesson and a detailed understanding of your methodology.
- 👍 Present new content in an organized, logical, and coherent manner that demonstrates knowledge of the subject matter and discipline.
- 👍 Design your instruction using contemporary principles of learning (anticipatory set, active engagement, closure), or the six components of explicit instruction (setting the stage, direct explanation, modeling, guided practice, independent practice, assessment of learning).
- 👍 Provide clear, thorough directions for tasks and utilize appropriate questioning techniques to ensure understanding before setting students to work.
- 👍 Smile.
- 👍 Provide for any and all opportunities for active student involvement.
- 👍 Show enthusiasm during instruction, demonstrate a positive outlook, show excitement for learning, and student success.
- 👍 Smile.
- 👍 Check for understanding.
- 👍 Provide closure by assessing learners' achievement of instructional objectives.
- 👍 Smile.

Insider Edge Note

If lecturing is the best or only instructional tool you have, don't even bother showing up to the interview. We suggest that the your teaching demonstration include two to three distinct instructional approaches depending upon time allotted and the nature of the strategies. Remember, the most important tests of teacher quality that these committees will be use will be whether candidates:

A. understand the cognitive processes that affect student learning and thinking; or put more simply "how students learn best."

B. successfully employ the strategies that maximize these processes resulting in outcomes such as understanding, memory and skill acquisition.

The Don'ts of the Teaching Demonstration

- ☠ Don't try to teach too much. It is likely that you will only have fifteen to twenty five minutes. Stay focused on the objective the committee gave you.
- ☠ Don't focus too much on classroom management. Remember, the principal and four other teachers are in the back of the room. This is usually not going to be an issue unless it is an intentionally contrived situation. If something arises, attend to it in a fluid, firm, but gracious manner.
- ☠ Do not use teacher-centered approaches the whole time.

Many committee members hold the teaching demonstration to be the most important factor in deciding which teaching candidate to select. As administrators who do the hiring, if we had to choose only one part of the process to determine who to hire, without hesitation, it would be the teaching demonstration. The responses to interview questions and resumes tell us something, but the demonstration is the closest opportunity we are going to get to see the actual product we will be investing in. Our advice is to prepare extensively, incorporate the very best practices you have been taught in your teaching program and then when you have put every piece in place you should enjoy the moment of teaching and be yourself.

> *As administrators who do the hiring, if we had to choose only one part of the process to determine who to hire, without hesitation, it would be the teaching demonstration.*

▌▌▌ Insider Edge Doc

The appendix to this book provides you with actual teaching demonstration tasks for each of the content areas. We also provide you with additional teaching demonstration rating tools. Take a trip to the appendix and find out what type of demonstration you might have to conduct, what principals and committees are looking for and how they are grading you!

Chapter

12

Portfolio Advice

Ok, let's take some time to talk about something that is often and incorrectly considered an add-on during teacher interviews: teaching portfolios. We strongly recommend that you do not show up for an interview without a portfolio. Every other candidate who meets with the interview team and who is competing with you for the job will bring one. And don't underestimate their value. These days, interview teams and principals expect them and use them as a determination of your qualifications, even if they don't look at them extensively, or at all!

> *These days, interview teams and principals expect [portfolios] and use them as a determination of your qualifications, even if they don't look at them extensively, or at all!*

The Hidden Power of Portfolios

After your interview is complete and you have left the room, committee members will often go around the table and rank your responses before they move on to the next candidate interview. Depending upon how the principal has organized the interviews, each member may have a chance to explain what their rating was for the question and why they chose to rate it in the way they did. This moment is a classic example of the "hidden power" of portfolios. One committee member will say something to the effect of, "well their answer on the assessment question just didn't explain all the aspects of assessment and I just feel that their response was very limited." Then another committee member will chime in and state something to the effect of, "while I agree with you, did you see their portfolio? They had traditional assessments, performance assessments, authentic assessments, little quick checks for understanding, etc. Once I saw their portfolio and realized that they clearly had the knowledge and competence in this area in addition to the experience of having actually implemented these strategies with their students, I raised their score on that question."

Many other committee members may follow this individual's lead and raise their grades for that question also. Our point is that this is just one example of the hidden benefits of the teaching portfolio in the interview. They can't be measured. They can't be planned. They can't be orchestrated. But, without a portfolio you lose this additional edge should the opportunity arise.

Insider Edge Note

Leave your portfolio, or at least a high quality copy of it, with the committee. Many building principals report that portfolios come back into play later in the interview process. Here's what happens. On the day of the interviews, principals are very busy managing the committee, ushering candidates in and out, etc. During this time, they have very little opportunity to peruse candidate's portfolios. But hours or even days later when the pool has been reduced to two or three, your portfolio could be resurrected to refersh their memory or break a tie. This is why we say, "leave your portfolio with the committee!" Principals and other decision makers will have it at their fingertips. If it is a tight competition between you and another candidate, your portfolio just might make the difference. The portfolio does not guarantee anything, but if you do not have one, you have missed a chance to increase your odds of landing the job.

10 things you must have or do when it comes to your portfolio

1. Have your portfolio held together in some way that looks professional. We have seen actual print shop bindings, leather three ring binders, artist portfolio cases etc. All are fine.

2. Be sure that your portfolio's overall interior appearance is consistent and properly reflects the investment that the district or school would be making in you.

3. Have some sort of system for organizing your portfolio and making it easy to navigate. For example you can create a table of contents with color coding and having colored tabs that also denote each section. This system should enable the reader to quickly get to the information they want to see about you.

4. Include an educational philosophy. Make this personal but short!

5. Include your resume or curriculum vitae.

6. Include a list of references with all supporting contact information.

7. Include five letters of recommendation. Make sure at least three of them have directly supervised you. The golden standard of reference letters are those that have been written by individuals who have supervised and evaluated you in the classroom (see chapter four of this book).

8. Include transcripts if you have a strong or good academic record. They can speak highly to your work ethic and preparation in a specific fashion that an interview sometimes cannot. Even if you do not offer them as a part of your portfolio, they are likely to be requested. If you have a poor academic record, your best hope is that everything else you did blew the committee out of the water and they will only use them in the human resources office to verify your degrees have been earned. However, if a committee is not eager to scrutinize the quality of your courses and performance, you might want to be concerned about the school or district you are joining. This is why we encourage you in the strongest terms to take your studies seriously if you are still working on a degree. The quality of courses and the grades you earn within those courses will have a far reaching impact.

9. Plan on the committee asking if they can keep your original portfolio and return it to you later. They may do this even if you have provided copies. We know this portfolio is a precious thing to you, but you are going to have to trust them with it and pick it up in a few hours or days if necessary. This may even give you another opportunity to informally speak with the principal when you pick it up.

10. Be sure that you review each and every artifact in the portfolio and ensure that there are no spelling or grammatical errors.

We have seen some amazing and creative teachers come up with interesting ideas on how to present themselves through a portfolio. The ideas and options are endless. In education, there is no set way to do a portfolio so use your imagination and adapt it to your own personality.

Here are some *great ideas we have seen that you may want to borrow when it comes to portfolios*:

- A statement of beliefs about curriculum, which was followed by examples of lessons, units, or projects that the candidate did with their students.

- A statement of beliefs about instruction, which was followed by photos of the candidate's classroom with their students in action to illustrate their lesson examples.

- Artifacts of student work. If possible it is impressive to include the lesson plan, task that you created for the students and the work that the student's produced.

- Some candidates have included classroom observation documents that they have received from an administrator. These, if you have them, can be powerful.

- A statement of beliefs about assessment followed by some sample assessments that the candidate had given to their students. This is a way to show that you have a full knowledge of the wide spectrum of assessment including traditional tests, authentic assessments, performance assessments, formative assessments, etc.

- A statement of beliefs about data followed with data that the candidate had generated and then used to inform their instruction.

- Evidence of continued professional development.
- Statement about classroom management theory and the steps that the teacher takes inside their classroom to create a safe and orderly environment.
- Candidates include final results of any projects or committees they have been a part of.
- Letters from parents commending the work you did with their children.
- Teachers hand the committee business cards with a website on it where the whole portfolio can be viewed.
- Video portfolios which show the candidate talking about teaching and their beliefs, the teacher in action with their students in their classrooms, the teacher coaching and working with students.
- A section purely dedicated to awards, honors, published works and recognition.

We cannot emphasize the power of pictures enough when it comes to portfolios. During interviews, committee members are trying to get to know you and trying to envision you teaching children. Don't trust their imaginations to do so, give them pictures. Pictures bring it together for committee members and verify the reality that you are meant to work with children. For this reason we recommend photos or newspaper articles of you:

- teaching students in the classroom.
- with students on field trips, learning excursions or outside class activities.
- with children while you are serving in advisor roles.
- with your students at musical or athletic events.
- coaching or working with children in a coaching capacity.
- as a leader and role model.

Final Do's and Don'ts

There are some basic 'do's and don'ts' that you have to be aware of when participating in teaching interviews. Throughout this book we have gone into these issues with some depth. This chapter is a quick summary that is of what you have learned in this book. Study this each time you head into an interview to stay on top of your game.

Interview Do's:
- Dress appropriately and be conservative.
- Be sure your personal grooming and cleanliness are impeccable.
- Know the exact time and location of your interview and know how long it takes to get there.
- Arrive at least 10 minutes prior to the start of the interview.
- Turn off your cell phone completely before you enter the building or leave it in the car.
- Smile.
- Treat everyone you meet with courtesy and respect. Their opinions of you might be solicited during hiring decisions.
- Offer a firm handshake, make eye contact, and have a friendly expression when someone from the interview team comes to greet you.

- Listen to your greeter's name and position. Try to remember it and the correct pronunciation.

- Address your interviewer by title (Ms., Mr., Dr.) and last name, even if your interviewer gives you a first and last name, until invited to do otherwise.

- Maintain good eye contact during the interview.

- Exhibit your intrinsic interest for working with children.

- Be sure you have memberships in professional organizations. Keep them current and uninterrupted.

- Sit still in your seat. Avoid fidgeting and slouching.

- Have confidence in using responses you have developed to The EDU Edge 'umbrella questions' and back up your statements with specific examples from your experiences whenever possible.

- Listen when members of the interview team are speaking and let them finish questions or statements completely.

- Be succinct in your responses.

- Pause for a moment and think before speaking if you need to, it's ok!

- Ask for clarification if you don't understand a question.

- Acknowledge if you do not know the answer to something. Be honest. Remember, it's ok to say, "I don't know."

- Treat the interview seriously and be sure that you are demonstrating that you are truly interested in the school and the position.

- Exhibit a positive attitude. Remember, the interview team is made up of teachers who are evaluating you as a potential colleague. Behave like someone with whom you would want to work.

- Only ask questions at the end of the interview if you have "good questions." If you do not ask questions, have a pleasant way to say this prepared ahead of time (see our recommendation on end of interview questions in chapter nine if you do not remember exactly what we are talking about here.)

- Be sure you understand the interview team's next step in the hiring process. If you can, find out when and from whom you should expect to hear next. And, know what action you are expected to take next, if any.

- Complete your research on the school community and its programs before the interview.

  ♣ When the committee chair concludes the interview, offer a firm handshake and make eye contact. Depart gracefully.

  ♣ Write a thank-you letter to your interviewer and get it in their hands within twenty-four hours.

  ♣ Be yourself.

OK, Now Here Are the Big Don'ts of the Interview Process:

  ☠ Don't falsify any application materials.

  ☠ Don't make excuses. Take responsibility for your decisions and your actions.

  ☠ Don't make unflattering comments about previous employers, districts, types of students, or professors. Education is a small closely knit group. People know each other and it is just bad etiquette. Even if they do not know the people or school you are talking about, this leaves the perception you are a negative person.

  ☠ Don't put the full court sales press on. Be confident in your skills, but not the sales person who won't leave people alone on the showroom floor.

  ☠ Don't ask about salary and benefits issues until the subject is brought up to you or you are offered the position.

  ☠ Don't give off topic or generic responses.

  ☠ Don't ramble and search for the correct answer. Think about what is being asked and respond the best you can in a concise manner. Value the committee's time. The interview highway is littered with those who have talked themselves out of a job.

  ☠ Don't act as though you are desperate for employment.

  ☠ Don't be lazy and unprepared for the typical interview questions. We have highlighted the 12 major domains for you to master the over 350 interview questions we have listed in the appendix of this book. It is all there for you. Practice makes perfect. Practice your responses and as you do, you will feel more and more comfortable.

  ☠ Don't try to guess what the committee wants to hear. Answer in a direct, honest but moderated manner. If your honest responses are that far off from what they want, it is likely that the situation would not have worked even if you were hired.

- ☠ Do not drop names of books, authors and educators unless they are appropriate to the question and you really know what you are talking about.
- ☠ Don't try to use connections to get the job. If they are there, they may naturally play a role, but if you try to push them on people or point them out, you will devalue your qualifications.
- ☠ Don't give the perception that you know everything about everything-even if you are a veteran teacher.
- ☠ Don't talk about your previous failures, exhibit frustrations, or demonstrate a negative attitude in an interview.
- ☠ Don't allow your cell phone to sound during the interview. Turn it off or leave it in your car.
- ☠ Don't interrupt, talk over or finish sentences for members of the interview team. Allow them to express themselves fully and end statements or questions without interjection.
- ☠ Don't panic about getting a job. Be patient, even if there are not many openings in your region. At the moment you think all hope is lost, one of the seeds you have planted may result in a call for an unexpected job. If your life's mission is to make a difference in the life of a child, you will find yourself in a classroom.

Again, these may seem like basics, but they are a must for all interviews. Review the 'Do's and Don'ts a day or so before you head into any interview so you will be confident and in good shape where others falter.

Chapter

14

Conclusion

Our team at The EDU Edge feels that there are few things more important than children. The teaching profession needs people that care about children and are willing to truly take the time to study and implement how students learn most effectively. If you are one of these people, we encourage you to be persistent in your pursuit of a teaching position, but also to be smart, even shrewd in your preparation. There are many factors you cannot control that determine whether you are selected for a teaching position so you must capitalize on the factors you can affect. You have already taken the first steps by acquiring this text. Learn from the interviews that are not successful and continue to use our resources as you head into additional interviews. Eventually you will land that job you want and will succeed at it if you have the skills and motivation. Please think of us as a partner in this process. Stop back to theEDUedge.com on a regular basis to see our latest resources and to let us know how we have affected your search for a teaching position.

Our very best to you in your search and in your career!

Bill & Mike

Appendix

Additional Candidate Screening Instruments

SCARHARBOR CITY SCHOOL DISTRICT
Telephone Reference Check Form

Candidate's Name		Title/Position	Date

Person Contacted	Company/School District	Phone	Completed by

1. When and for how long did (Name of Candidate) work for you?
   Dates _____ Total in Yrs/Mos _____
2. How well did (Name of Candidate) relate to Supervisors? Teachers? Peers? Parents? Students?

   _____4. Very well – all groups   _____2. Some problems - may not have been his/her fault.
   _____3. Very well – most groups   _____1. Overall, not very well

3. On a scale of 1 to 4, with 4 being the highest, please rate (Name of Candidate) characteristics in the following areas in comparison to the top performers in your district/organization:

Charcteristic	Rating	Characteristic	Rating	Characteristic	Rating
Flexibility		Communication Skills		Knowledge of content	
Punctuality/Attendance		Leadership		Organizational skills	
Lesson Planning		Enthusiasm		Morality/Integrity/Honesty	
Class Management					

4. How does (Name of Candidate) respond to suggestions for change/constructive criticism?

   _____4. Always listens and   _____2. Listening and/or follow through okay
       follows through   but could be better
   _____3. Usually listens and   _____1. Does not respond well
       follows through

5. Based upon the scale of 1 to 4, with 4 being the highest, how would you rate (Name of Candidate) in the performance of his/her duties in comparison to the top performers in your district/organization:
   _____ 4. Outstanding _____ 3. Above Average _____ 2. Average _____ 1. Fair
6. Using the same scale, how would you rate the degree to which you'd want (Name of Candidate) to work with your own children?

       1   2   3   4
   Lowest   Highest
7. Do you have any additional comments or reservations about (name)?

Overall Rating (average of 1-6 above) to be completed by administrator conducting the reference check:

PLEASANT VALLEY CITY SCHOOL DISTRICT
Teacher Telephone Reference Checklist

Candidate: _____   Administrator: _____   Date: _____

Person Contacted: _____
Position / Title: _____

1. What are some of the strong characteristics (positive / negative) of this candidate?

2. How does this candidate interact with students?   Staff members?   Parents?

3. To what degree does this teachers become involved in school activities and projects?

4. How does this teacher demonstrate creative teaching techniques?

5. How has this candidate consistently demonstrated acceptable levels of planning for classroom instruction?

ABC Central School District
Candidate Assessment Form

This form is to be completed following the interviews of candidates for any/all positions-administrators, supervisors, teachers and support staff. Develop and ask similar, relevant, experience-based questions of all candidates for the position. Generally speaking, in addition to the basic competencies associated with the job postings, job description, and evaluation criteria for the position, each successful candidate should possess/display **character** (e.g., work ethic, interest in the position/District and "student centeredness") **content knowledge** (e.g. knowledge/experience that address the expectations for the position), and **special skills** (e.g. skills and experiences that go above and beyond basic competency). Assess the candidate **holistically,** considering application materials, results of initial references checks and interview. Complete and sign the form, adding it to the folder of each applicant interviewed.

Strengths:

Weaknesses:

Concerns/Unknown:

Committee Member Signatures:

LINCOLN CENTRAL SCHOOL DISTRICT
<u>Teacher Candidate Process</u>
Teaching Demonstration Lesson Checklist

Candidate: _____

Administrator: _____ **Date:** _____

Demo School: _____ **Grade level:** _____

2	1	0
exceeds expectations	meets expectations	below expectations (not observed)

Instructional Skills:

_____ Follows appropriate curriculum
_____ Uses effective planning
_____ States specific objective
_____ Has knowledge of subject matter
_____ Assesses learning
_____ Provides examples
_____ Uses motivational strategies
_____ Shows enthusiasm
_____ Provides opportunities for practice
_____ Provides opportunities for active student involvement
_____ Uses effective questioning
_____ Adapts instruction to various abilities
_____ Relates instruction to student interest
_____ Demonstrates sensitivity to students
_____ Uses technology in instructional process

Management Skills:

_____ Establishes procedures that promote learning
_____ Makes effective use of time
_____ Encourages positive interaction
_____ Uses appropriate disciplinary techniques

Professional Skills:

_____ Professional appearance
_____ Voice
_____ Articulation
_____ Punctuality

Total Points: _____
Notes:

Examples of Written Tasks

English Language Arts Example

In Kate Chopin's *The Awakening* (1899), protagonist Edna Pontellier is said to possess "That outward existence which conforms, the inward life that questions." In a novel or play that you have studied, identify a character who outwardly conforms while questioning inwardly. Then write an essay in which you analyze how this tension between outward conformity and inward questioning contributes to the meaning of the work. Avoid mere plot summary.

Mathematics Example

The principal of this school is visiting math classrooms at different levels to see the difference between the material being presented. As she goes from class to class, she looks for progression from beginning level grade 9 mathematics (Basic factoring) to AP Calculus class (Integration). This is what she sees:

-In one 9th grade class students were factoring a trinomial

   For example: 15ax4 + 5a2x3 + 10ax

      5ax (3x3 + ax2 + 2)

-In another class students had a more advanced type of factoring:

   Example 1: Find the value of (x2 – 5x + 4) if x = 7

   Example 2: Express x2 + 5x – 6 as the product of two binomials.

-In another class students were solving logarithmic equations

   For example: log 4 (m-1) + log 4 (m-1) = 2

         log 4 (m-1) (m-1) = 2

         log 4 (m2-2m + 1) = 2

-And an AP Calculus class was integrating equations like:

For example: $\int_{-2}^{2} /x^2 - 1/\, dx \;=\; \int_{-2}^{-2} (x^2 - 1)dx + \int_{1}^{2} (x^2 - 1)dx \;-\; \int_{-1}^{1} (x^2 - 1)dx$

In a well written essay, please explain (1) in your opinion, if this reflects the proper progression of mathematics instruction, (2) aligns with the State's mathematics curriculum, and (3) what level you feel most capable of teaching and why.

Social Studies Example

Please develop a lesson plan surrounding one of the following content topics: (1) Comparisons and Contrasts between West African Civilizations or (2) The Rise of the Labor Movement and Labor Organizations in the United States. List steps that you would take to determine which students are struggling with this content and steps you would take to assist those who are.

Science Example

Please use the next thirty minutes to design a lesson that teaches how the following influenced the origin of living organisms: (a) Photosynthesis (b) Oxygen and the Ozone Layer (c) Endosymbiotic theory. Your lesson should include state standards AND key ideas. Include a brief summary for each influence listed above. Please discuss any differences you would anticipate in how you would deliver this lesson to a Biology class versus an Evolution class?

Second Language Example

* Note – Principals across the country report that because very few of them speak a second language, they ask the department chair to: (1) ask questions during the interview in the target language to assess their speaking and listening skills and (2) ask the department chair to assess their writing skills in the target language. From our research and experience the vast majority of the time this means answering a typical interview question in the target language.

Please respond to the following question in French. You will have 30 minutes to complete your response. Please add accents or characters not provided by the software program by hand.

AP English Example

The following is a prompt and a student response from the 2005 AP Literature Examination. Your task is to read the student essay and provide assessment on the writing. If you were conferencing with the student on this piece, what would your comments be? Your written response may take any form that is most comfortable to you (i.e. bullet points, dialogue, paragraph form).

A symbol is an object, action, or event that represents something or that creates a range of associations beyond itself. A symbol can express an idea, clarify meaning, or enlarge literal meaning.

Select a novel or a play and, focusing on one symbol, write an essay analyzing how that symbol functions in the work and what it reveals about the characters or themes of the work as a whole.

Special Education Example

1. Please completely address the following two items to the best of your ability. You will be provided with 30 minutes to work on this task.

(A) A student on the autism continuum may present with symptoms such as rigidity, perseveration and restricted patterns of behavior. Describe strategies that you may utilize in your classroom if a student is "stuck" on a specific topic or behavior. How might you re-engage a student back to task?

(B) One of your students has limited verbal abilities. What techniques might you use to elicit responses from him and include him in your classroom activities?

2. Please use the next thirty minutes to develop a lesson plan explaining to a class of high school level autistic students what a document based question is and how you successfully respond to such questions. Indicate the adaptations and modifications you would make to lesson planning to accommodate for the specific needs of this population.

Music Example

Please complete the following tasks to the best of your ability. You will be provided with 30 minutes to work on this task.

Realize the figured bass below in four voices, following traditional eighteenth-century voice-leading procedures. Continue logically from the spacing of the first chord. Do not add embellishments unless indicated by the figured bass. In the space below each chord, supply the Roman numeral that appropriately indicates harmonic function.

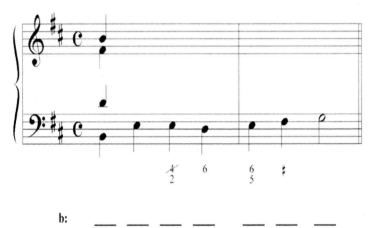

Write the following progression in four voices, following the eighteenth-century voice-leading procedures. Continue logically from the spacing of the first chord. Do not add embellishments unless indicated by the Roman and Arabic numerals. Use only quarter and half notes.

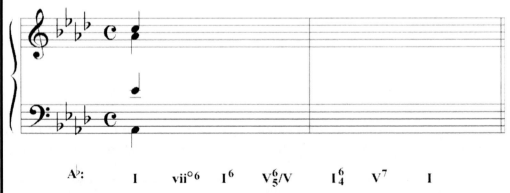

Advanced Placement or International Baccalaureate Coordinator Example

Write a one-page introductory letter to the faculty introducing yourself and detailing your vision for the future of the program. This letter may be an opportunity to entice faculty members who have previously struggled to understand how to implement the program within their classroom or have demonstrated no interest in the program.

School Counselor Example

The attached transcript belongs to Sally B. Good entering Grade 12. The parents of this student have asked you to advise them on what remaining courses their child needs during senior year to arrive at:

A. State Diploma
B. Courses that will help them to arrive at a career in accounting.
C. Courses that will help her to gain admission to the school she would like to attend which is Ithaca College.
D. Goals and Strategies that will help her to earn SAT scores needed to arrive at these goals.

Please use the next 45 minutes to analyze the transcript and write a letter to these parents responding to this inquiry/providing advice. A laptop computer has been made available to create this letter. Our office staff will assist you in printing this document at the end of your 45 minutes.

Business Education Example

1. The position that you are applying demands someone that has a strong accounting background. The successful candidate will be responsible for teaching our Advanced Accounting students. In a well-developed and organized essay, please explain the accounting concepts and practices related to notes receivable, unearned revenue, and accrued revenue?

2. The position that you are applying for is part of our High School's Finance Academy. The successful candidate will have to teacher one required course (Academy of Finance – Success Strategies) and oversee the Academy's

internship program. In a well-written essay, please describe the habits commonly found in successful teens and then analyze the steps that you would take to ensure that Academy students incorporate them into their internship experience.

Visual Art Example*

1. Many would conclude that Frida Kahlo's work is a visual narrative of her life. In the next 45 minutes, in a well-written essay, please describe a unit that you would use to teach on Frida Kahlo's work and how it applies to the elements and principles of art. Please include:

(a) the events that became repeated themes in her painting? Why is this important?

(b) the different images she created reflected about her life? How does this apply?

(c) how Kahlo used the elements and principles throughout her work? What does this mean for your students and their learning?

* From our research, writing tasks in Visual Art seem to have a heavy emphasis on the teacher's content knowledge and how the teacher's content knowledge will be applied to their students' learning.

Physical Education

There are seven personal and social health skills that students need to know and be able to do to be safe, healthy and achieve the State and National Standards.

A.   Please describe the benefits of the skills-driven approach NYS adopted in 2005 as a part of the Navigate by the Stars Health Initiative.

B.   To the best of your ability, describe the standards you would expect to teach within three of the seven skill areas:

- Self-Management
- Relationship Management
- Stress Management
- Communication
- Planning and Goal Setting
- Decision Making

· Advocacy
C.   Describe how each of the three skill areas you selected might be utilized in a skill based learning opportunity.

Additional General Topic Written Task

(We have seen this one pop up in a number of school districts we studied- whether it comes out in the interview or written task- be ready for it!)

Describe a lesson that you have delivered in the past that you consider a failure. Have you been able to analyze/diagnose why it was ineffective? If so, describe your conclusions and how this helped your instruction to improve from that point on.

Teacher Interview Questions:
The 12 Domains and Umbrella Questions (UQ)

Domain 1: Beginning of Interview – Ice Breakers
   1. **UQ- Tell us a little about yourself both personally and professionally.**
   2. Welcome…. Begin by telling us a little about yourself, your experience and background.
   3. What three words would you use to describe yourself? And Why?
   4. Describe yourself and your teaching experiences.
   5. Tell us about yourself.
   6. Tell us about yourself and your experiences working with students at this age level.

Domain 2: About You Personally – Who Are You?
   1. **UQ- What personal qualities will contribute to your success as a teacher?**
   2. What special qualities do you bring to this job?
       OR What do you believe qualifies you for this position?
       OR What skills and abilities make you an ideal candidate for the position?
       OR What would you like us to know about you before we begin?
   3. Describe your educational and student teaching experiences.
       OR Give me one or two examples of things that you discovered about yourself while student teaching/prior teaching experiences that you would like to improve.
       OR Describe your student teaching experience. What are the most significant things that you learned from your cooperating teacher?
   4. How would your cooperating teacher describe you?
       OR How do you think your family and friends would describe you?
   5. What part of this job are you looking forward to?
       OR What part of this job scares you?
   6. Describe your organizational style.

OR Being organized is important. Give us an example of how you organize yourself.

OR How organized are you?

OR Why do you think organization is an important quality for a teacher to possess?

7. What do you see yourself doing in 5, 10, 20, 30 years?

8. Tell us one thing we should know about you.

9. Tell me about a situation when you had to learn something new in a short time. How did you do this?

10. Describe the biggest challenge you've ever had to face.

OR How have you most constructively dealt with disappointment and turned it into a learning experience?

OR Describe a personal experience, which had an impact on your teaching.

11. What were you like as a student?

OR were you a good student?

OR Do you think that it is important for a teacher to have been a good student?

12. Describe your ability to listen and be responsive. Can you give me an example?

13. What are your strengths and weaknesses?

14. What motivates you personally and professionally?

15. If you were criticized for something you did right, how would you handle this?

16. Are you the kind of person children and adults confide in? What makes you think so?

17. Do you think you are a flexible person? Explain.

18. Do you consider yourself a risk taker? Give an example.

19. Are you a positive and energetic person?

20. Which type of student do you think you work best with (At-risk; low, moderate, high academic achievement)?

21. What are your interests outside teaching?

22. Tell us about yourself as it relates to the position.

Domain 3: Professionalism & The Teaching Profession

1. **UQ- Who has been your greatest teaching mentor? What characteristics make him/her a good teacher?**

2. What are the qualities of an excellent teacher? Which of these qualities do you have?
   OR What attributes are common to good teaching?
   OR What do you consider the most critical elements in the successful performance of your position?

3. What/who influenced you the most to become a teacher?
   OR Why did you choose education as your career?
   OR Why do you want to become a teacher?
   OR Why did you choose the teaching profession as a career?

4. What are your greatest strengths as a teacher? Greatest weaknesses?

5. What do you do to keep up with current trends/innovative strategies in instruction and assessment?
   OR How do you stay current in your field?

6. How will you insure that you continue to improve/develop as a teacher over the next 5, 10, 30 years?

7. What is your philosophy of education?
   OR What is the purpose of education?

8. How have you evaluated you own teaching to improve?

9. Tell me about a time where a student or a class taught you something.

10. What was the last book that your read?
    OR What books are you currently reading?
    OR What journal articles have you read in the last six months?

11. What are the greatest challenges facing public education today?
    OR what are the biggest changes that will impact education over the next three years?
    OR In your opinion, what are the biggest challenges that teachers face today?
    OR What are some of the greatest challenges of being an educator?
    OR What is the most exciting initiative happening in your area of education today?

      OR If you had the authority and resources to change one thing in education, what would it be? Why?

12. Describe one time when you've acted as a leader.

      OR Summarize a situation where you had to generate a new idea or suggestion and tell me about how you got this idea implemented.

13. Describe a professional mistake that you have made. Discuss what you have learned from the experience.

14. What do you like most and least about your current or last position?

15. How would you resolve problems with your administration?

      OR Describe a situation where you had to work with a difficult supervisor, professor, or other person. How did you successfully interact with this person?

      OR How do you feel about disagreement among professionals?

      OR If your school had a concern, how would you go about solving it? What should a principal expect from teachers? What should teachers expect from their principal?

      OR How would you expect your principal to help you?

16. Describe what colleagueship and collaboration should look like among teachers.

      OR Describe a team project you have done and your role.

      OR How would you describe your interactions or orientation toward others?

      OR Give an example of a time when you've worked on a team.

      OR How do you view your interpersonal relationships with students, staff, parents, and community?

17. What quality or qualities do you have that would enhance our teaching staff?

18. Describe you experience teaching in an urban, rural, or suburban setting?

19. What kinds of in-services would you be eager to attend?

      OR What professional teaching organizations do you belong to?

      OR what are your plans for professional growth?

Domain 4: Beliefs on Curriculum & Planning

1. **UQ- What do you feel are the most important things students learn in your classroom?**
2. Describe the components of an effective lesson plan.
   OR What four key components do you believe you must include in your plan?
   OR Can you show us what your lesson plan book would look like?
3. What do you need to know in order to begin your lesson planning for a class?
4. What are some considerations you make when planning you lessons? How do you plan for a unit?
5. Do you use thematic units?
   OR What is an example of a recent thematic unit used in your classroom?
6. Describe two curricular topics that you have taught in this grade/subject area.
7. How do you balance the need to prepare students for our state tests while at the same time provide meaningful and engaging instruction?
8. Explain what a strong balanced literary program would look like in your classroom.
9. What have you done to start and to end a class successfully?
10. Some of your students always finish their assignments early. How would you deal with the free time that they have?
11. Describe a high-interest project that you might assign to your students.
12. How have state standards and curriculum for this subject guided your teaching?
    OR How do you make sure you are teaching to the state standards?
13. Do you see yourself initiating any cross-curricular projects with other teachers? If so, what types of program /project would you envision implementing?
14. How would you involve the community in your classroom?
15. How can you make your teaching connect to students' real-world experiences?
    OR What do you see as the link between _____ and preparation for the real world?

16. How do you motivate students?
    OR How would you motivate the reluctant learner?
17. What does the term school improvement mean to you?
18. What instructional strategies would you use to incorporate writing, reading, and math across the curriculum?
19. Tell us what you know about learning styles and how you will address them in your classroom?
20. Please give us a specific example of a lesson and how it addressed different learning styles.
21. Name a book that you'd like to read to (or with) your students. Describe the book and tell why you chose it.
22. How have you incorporated multiculturalism/diversity in your classroom in the past? How do you plan to do this at this school?
    OR Describe your experiences working with a diverse student body.
    OR In what ways can you teach students to be accepting of one another?
    OR What specific approaches or ideas have you used in dealing with at-risk students?

Domain 5: Beliefs on Instruction

1. **UQ- Describe a lesson that worked exceptionally for you. Why do you think it succeeded?**
2. **UQ- Describe a lesson that you consider a failure. Have you been able to analyze/diagnose why it was ineffective?**
3. Describe the ideal classroom.
    OR If I walked by your classroom and I looked through the window into your classroom, what would I see?
4. Name a specific method or strategy you have used to teach in the past and why it is one that you will continue to use?
5. How do you feel students learn best?
    OR What four words would students use to describe your teaching strategies?
6. Are there learning centers in your classroom? How have you used them? Describe.

7. Do you have some samples of past lesson you have taught that we could view?
8. Name a few student-centered instructional strategies that you subscribe to.
9. How do you teach kids to use higher order thinking in your classroom?
10. How do you make learning fun for your students?
11. How do you engage students in their learning?
    OR What techniques would you use to keep students actively involved and motivated during a lesson?
12. What two core teaching strategies do you use to achieve your desired results?
13. Give an example of how you have used cooperative learning in your classroom.
    OR Define cooperative learning and give an example of how you have used it.
14. How would you decide on groups? What are your beliefs in this regard?
15. Do you prefer homogeneous or heterogeneous grouping? Why?
16. Are there any strategies that you use to encourage teamwork among your students?
17. How do you reinforce self-esteem in students?
    OR If a student fails, what would be your feeling or reaction?
    OR How do you provide support for students who are not performing as well as they should?
23. Tell us about a lesson where you had to differentiate your instruction.
    OR How do you provide remediation and acceleration within your classroom?
    OR What does individualized teaching mean to you?
    OR Describe how you have differentiated a lesson to accommodate varying student needs.
    OR What provisions do you make for meeting the range of skills and needs commonly present in a classroom?
18. How would you instruct students who perform below grade level, especially those from disadvantaged socio-economic backgrounds?
19. What can you do for a student that is extremely gifted?

20. How do you feel about technology in the classroom?
    OR How would you incorporate technology into your classroom?
    OR What software have you used for instructional purposes?
21. How would you go about relating to your students?
22. What daily or weekly routines would be incorporated into your teaching?
23. Do you feel that drill and practice are important? How and when would you use it in your teaching?
24. Describe a part of your portfolio that best indicates your teaching style and beliefs and tell us how you have implemented this in the classroom.
25. How do you keep students on task?
    OR What would you do with a student that was off task?
26. In what ways do you encourage creativity in your classroom?
27. What are effective instructional strategies that motivate students toward active participation in the learning process?
    OR Describe the types of instructional strategies you would use to facilitate learning and to ensure total involvement and active participation of all students.
    OR How do you increase the chances that students will understand what you are teaching?
28. How do you feel about noise in your classroom?
29. What research-based teaching strategies have you used?
30. Describe your homework policy/philosophy.
    OR What would you do with students who fail continually to complete homework?
    OR How much homework will you assign? How do you go about measuring how long it will take your students?

Domain 6: Beliefs on Assessment

1. **UQ- Define the term assessment and tell us what strategies are most effective for assessing student progress?**
2. Describe your grading/assessment policy/philosophy.
3. What are your feelings about state and standardized testing?
4. How will you determine if students are learning?

OR What evaluation techniques do you use?

OR How do you measure student performance in your classroom?

OR What kinds of tests do you like to give?

OR Describe the types of quizzes, tests, projects that you give.

OR In a quarter, what types of evaluations compose your quarterly report?

OR Describe the type of tests and quizzes that you promote.

5. While the lesson is going on, how can you tell if students are getting the material?

   OR If you are teaching a lesson and your students don't seem to be "getting it", what do you do?

   OR How can you tell students are learning?

   OR What would you do if 50% of the students in your class did poorly on a test?

   OR Describe a time when a lesson was not going well. What did you do about it?

6. Have you ever been required to design lesson plans around a specific rubric? If so, what did it consist of?

7. How should a student's educational achievement and progress be measured?

8. What do you do to prepare your students for state or standardized tests?

9. How do you provide feedback to students about how they are doing?

   OR How important is feedback to student success?

10. What would you do if students were not able to answer your questions?

11. How would you find out about students' attitudes and feelings regarding your class?

12. How do you know whether your curriculum is appropriately matched to your students' needs?

Domain 7: Classroom Management

1. **UQ- What does classroom management mean to you? Please describe the process that you have used in dealing with a student who was disrupting the class.**
2. Describe your approach for student behavior management and how you could prevent disruptive behavior in the classroom.
    OR Describe a classroom management plan that you have used and why it worked?
    OR Describe your classroom management style. How would you set up a student management system?
    OR what steps would you take with a student who is disruptive in the classroom?
    OR What kind of classroom management plan do you like best and how would you implement it?
3. What is the difference between rules and routines as it applies to classroom management? Which would we be more likely to find in your classroom?
4. At what point do you involve the principal in a discipline matter?
5. What are the rules of your classroom? How are they established?
6. What kind of relationship do you have with your students?
7. What kind of learning environment do you try to create?
8. Some people say that you should command respect. Do you agree or disagree?
9. If a student said that you were the worst teacher she ever had, what would you say?
10. How do you make students feel at ease around you, while still respecting you?
11. How do you show your students that you understand them and their frustrations?
12. When students say they want their teacher to be "fair," what do you think they mean?
13. How do you resolve conflict between people?
    OR How would you teach conflict resolution to your students?
14. Is it appropriate to tell your class that you are angry with them?

15. Describe some methods of "positive reinforcement" that you might use in your classroom.
16. What are some ways that you can avoid behavior problems?
17. How do you get students to do what you want them to do?
18. How do you handle children who are difficult to manage?
19. Describe the toughest discipline situation you encountered and how you handled it.
    OR similar question followed by … In hindsight, would you have handled this situation differently?
20. If you were having classroom management difficulties, when and who would you ask for help?
21. Do you ever feel angry toward your students?
22. Why do students act out in class?
23. What is your attitude towards individual vs. total class punishment?
24. Who should be responsible for the discipline in the school?
25. How would you create a behavior modification plan for a student with on-going behavior problems?
26. What is the most difficult aspect of discipline for you?
27. Would you describe yourself as a tough teacher or an understanding teacher?
28. Expect a variety of scenario questions and how you would handle them:
    - What would you do if a student was consistently late to your class?
    - What would you do if a student refused to do the work that you assigned?
    - What would you do if a student complained about an assignment that you had given?
    - What would you do if a student wasn't handing his/her homework on a regular basis?
    - What would you do if a student was chronically tired and sleeping in your class?
    - What would you do if one student hit another student?
    - What would you do if a student was swearing in your class?

- What would you do to handle subtle or covert student to student bullying?
- What would you do if you were teaching a class and a student just stood up and walked around the room? Next, the student refuses and says, "Make me you …." What do you do then?
- What would you do if a student was belligerent, defiant, and refused to leave your classroom and go to the main office when instructed to do so?

Domain 8: Special Education

1. **UQ- Have you worked with special education students in the past? In what capacity? How do you balance the special requirements of students with IEPs with the needs of the remainder of your students?**
2. How would you use teacher aides and parent volunteers?
3. How would you work with a mainstreamed learning-disabled student?
4. How do you feel about students who are mainstreamed into your class?
5. Have you worked within a team setting before in delivering services? What strengths and experience do you bring to our team setting in this regard?
6. How would you go about recommending a child for special education services? What would you have done beforehand and in preparation?
7. How do you feel about working in an inclusion classroom?
8. How do you meet the needs of a student with an IEP?
9. What is your approach to working with mainstream teachers as your students push into classes that are appropriate?
10. What do you know about working with students with Aspergers? What experience do you have in this area?
11. To what degree have you been involved in CSE meetings? Describe your experiences and how you can best help the process and student?
12. Are you familiar with the consultant teacher model? What are some of the different ways in which the consultant is used in the general ed. classroom?
13. Are you familiar with co-teaching? What are your feelings about co-teaching with a Special Educator?

Domain 9: Content Knowledge

1. **UQ- Where do your true interests/passions lie within your content area? (Elementary teachers, we recommend that you focus your thinking and preparation on Reading.)**

Elementary

2. Describe the ideal reading program.
   OR What reading programs do you have experience with?
   OR What approaches to teaching reading have you used?
3. What is guided reading?
4. What are the components of a balanced literacy program?
   OR How would you incorporate phonics into a balanced literacy program?
5. If you were hired to teach starting this September, how would you go about setting up your reading program?
6. You are certified to teach in K-6 grades, choose a specific grade level and describe your literacy program that you believe will meet the needs of all of your learners.
   OR Most classes have students with a wide range of reading abilities. What can you do to meet the needs of students with high reading abilities and low reading abilities at the same time?
7. What would you do if a parent called upset that their child was placed in the "wrong" reading group?
8. During literacy time in your classroom, what are you doing? What are the children doing?
9. How have you used manipulatives in teaching math?

Secondary

2. What courses within your content area do you feel most comfortable teaching?
   OR Which curriculum area do you feel you are particularly strong in?
   OR What is your educational background and teaching experience related to the subject area that you want to teach?
3. What coursework have you taken that you feel has made you an especially competent teacher in your area?

4. What goals do you hope to achieve in your subject?

Domain 10: Knowledge of School/District – School Pride

1. **UQ- Why do you want to teach at this school?**
2. Why do you want to teach in this, particular district?
3. What do you know about us?
4. What can you offer our school that other candidates cannot?
5. With which extra-curricular programs are you interested in getting involved?
   OR Which extra-curricular programs do you have experience with? And, which one are you interested in if you became part of our school?
   OR Which extra-curricular activities are you most interested in supervising?
6. Why are you the right fit for our school?
   OR Why should our school/district choose you?
7. What community activities would you like to be associated with? Why?

Domain 11: Parent Communication & Building Relationships

1. **UQ- How would you involve parents in their child's academic/discipline problems at school?**
2. Parent communications are a very important component of classroom success.   Please share what forms of communication you have (or will) implement in your classroom.
   OR How do you engage a parent in the education of his or her child?
   OR How do you keep parents informed of their child's progress?
   OR What instruments will you employ to insure the highest level of communication with parents at our school?
   OR Describe positive communications with parents and families that you have used in the past.
   OR Describe some ways you can inform parents of what is going on in your classroom.
3. Are parent/teacher conferences important? Why or why not?

OR In your opinion, how effective are parent conferences in solving student problems?

4. What steps have you taken prior to a parent-teacher conference to ensure success?
5. In what ways do you communicate with parents on a regular basis?
6. Do you have an example of a parent newsletter that you can show us?
7. A parent calls you because they are worried about their child's low grades. What would you say to the parent?
8. A parent writes a note and tells you that their daughter could not complete their homework assignment because she had a piano recital the night before. What do you do?
9. What would you do if a parent complained about an assignment that you had given?
10. Describe the reasons why you would contact parents.
11. How would you handle making a difficult phone call to a parent?
12. What would you include in your Open House presentations to parents?
13. Tell me some ways you would involve parents in your classroom.
14. How would you use teacher aides and parent volunteers?
15. What would you do to calm an angry parent?

Domain 12: End of Interview

1. **UQ- What questions do you have for us?**
2. What things about yourself would you like to bring out that have not been brought out in the interview?
3. What were you hoping we might ask today, but did not?

Teaching Demonstration Scenarios

English Languages Arts Example

The Situation: Your AP Literature students have had some difficulty with **embedding quotations** within their analytical writing assignments. *Your Task:* Prepare and then teach a lesson no longer than 15 minutes on effectively using quotations from works of literature to support analytical writing.

Math Examples

1. Prepare and then teach a lesson on Unit Circle (Trigonometry) no longer than 20 minutes.
2. You are teaching an algebra lesson to 6 students on the autism continuum. Your objective for the lesson is to teach them what ratios are and how to determine whether ratios form a proportion. The students range in ability from 7th grade level to a 9th grade level ages 15-18 years old. Write a lesson plan that details appropriate modifications and accommodations that will meet individual needs of your students.

Social Studies Example

1. Please be prepared to begin your meeting with the committee by presenting a lesson no longer than 15 minutes on one of the following topics: Major Changes and Continuities in Formation of National Identity in Southeast Asia: 1914 to Present Or … Jacksonian Democracy: Theory, Reality, and Relationship to American Political Foundations from 1607 to 1815

Science

1. Prepare and teach a lesson on Protein Synthesis: Translation. The lesson should be no longer than 20 minutes and should get students actively engaged in meaningful work.
2. Prepare a Regents Earth Science lesson that teaches students about weathering erosion and deposition of particles in a stream bed. Be sure to apply to streambeds with meanders and straightaways.

Music Example

For a class of Music Theory I students: Present a lesson on *hearing* the *ascending diatonic intervals* based on the major scale using the tonic as the lower pitch. Assume the students are already familiar with the major scale. Focus on helping students develop strategies to aurally recognize each interval. Include a brief evaluative activity.

Second Language Example

1. Compare and Contrast the Usage of the "imparfait" vs. "passé composé" tenses for a class of French II students. Have students interact with these tenses and check for understanding at the end of your instruction.

2. We are presently studying a unit on _____. Using a communicative approach to second language instruction, please get students listening to and speaking in the target language.

Technology Examples

1. Go through basic intro lesson plan on the steps to designing and setting up a new website (include planning, structure, software used, explain how to get your own domain, etc).
2. Run through intro lesson plan on introduction to computers, include hardware and software aspects of a computer system, maybe have a computer on hand for the teacher to demonstrate various parts and how they all work together.
3. Several of our web classes involve Macromedia products (Flash, Dream Weaver, etc). Please teach a basic lesson on what is flash, how it is used, any do a quick demo with the software.

Advanced Placement/International Baccalaureate Coordinator Example

You have been hired as IB (or AP) Coordinator at Lincoln School. You have been asked to give a presentation to a group of several families considering our school for their children. Both parents and students are present for this gathering. Families should not only be given a general understanding of the program, but the benefits of participation.

Business Example

The Accounting 1 class you are about to teach is presently on Chapter 14 "Preparing Payroll Records" of their Textbook: South-Western Century 21 Accounting First-Year, General Journal Approach Sixth Edition Ross, Hanson, Gilbertson, Lehman & Swanson. Please plan a lesson where at the conclusion, students understand and can explain the accounting concepts and practices related to calculating payroll?

Art Example

Most common among art teaching demonstrations:
Teach a lesson on contour line drawing.

Other Examples:
Please be prepared to begin your meeting with the committee by delivering a lesson no longer than 15 minutes on the following topic:

- *Example #1* = 7th Grade - How value techniques improve the three-dimensional quality in portrait drawings
  ### OR
- *Example #2* = 8th Grade - Why complementary mixing (color theory) is essential to landscape painting?
  ### OR
- *Example #3* = Studio in Art - What the devices are and why we use them to create the illusion of depth?

<u>Physical Education</u>

Please be prepared to begin your meeting with the committee by delivering a lesson no longer than 15 minutes on the following topic:

POST EXERCISE STRETCHING REGIMEN WITH PHYSIOLOGICAL EXPLANATION

Please feel free to incorporate the feel and structure that would be typical of your teaching style for grade nine. Our committee will serve as your students. The classroom we will use includes a dry-erase board should you need it. If you are in need of any additional equipment or technology in order to deliver your lesson, please contact Mrs. Quack at 888-4444 and we will attempt to make arrangements.

Acknowledgements

It is crucial that we acknowledge the incredible support from our highly intelligent, beautiful and superhuman wives. They have provided us with the time and understanding to meet the demands of our school communities. On top of this, they bought into our belief that as authors we could assist an even wider group of individuals often left with little support when it comes to the intimidating and secretive process of teacher hiring. If you are finding this book useful, it is because Carol Vallely and Kelly Kresse supported us during its production.

Kathy Rogers of K. Corff Design was a constant resource with design and image issues surrounding the creation of The EDU Edge several years ago as well as this first book.

Tandy Hamilton gave us last minute heroics as a narrator of the audiobook and also lent us her thoughtful copy editing skills.

John Cotton of frugalaudio.com made recording the audiobook version of this text a pleasure. His magic as a sound engineer and advice on digital audio distribution was invaluable.

Bob Gallagher of Buffalo State College provided direct and genuine feedback on our manuscript.

Thank you to the hundreds of school administrators who responded to our inquiries for interview tasks, questions and systems artifacts over the past few years as we have been compiling this book. Your time and generosity may very well produce stronger candidates for your committees to review and will make someone, somewhere more comfortable and confident on interview day.

About the Authors

Bill Kresse has served as a school counselor, social studies teacher, assistant principal and principal in a variety of settings including rural, urban, private, and public schools. Since 2005 he has served as principal of City Honors School in Buffalo, NY. Under Dr. Kresse's leadership, City Honors has regularly been named as one of the top public schools in the United States by *Newsweek*, *The Washington Post* and *US News and World Report*. He recently led the school through a multi-year process of planning, construction and relocation of its nine hundred students and staff to undergo a forty million dollar restoration and expansion of its historic facility. He holds an undergraduate degree in history and government from Georgetown University, a masters degree in education from Canisius College, and masters and Ph.D. degrees in school administration from Cornell University. Dr. Kresse has been acknowledged with the Allen Secondary Education Leadership Award from the School Administrators Association of New York State (SAANYS), the New York State Assistant Principal Excellence Award from SAANYS, the '40 under 40' Award from *Business First Magazine* and was a Bezos Scholar. He resides in Buffalo, NY with his wife and two sons.

Mike Vallely has served as a Spanish teacher, assistant principal, principal, director of secondary education and assistant superintendent in rural and suburban settings. Since 2006, he has served as assistant superintendent for Curriculum, Instruction and Pupil Personnel Services of Lancaster Central Schools in Lancaster, NY. Under Dr. Vallely's leadership, the district has seen an unprecedented improvement in student performance, graduation rates and students taking advanced level courses. He holds an undergraduate degree in education from Buffalo State College, a masters degree in interdisciplinary studies from Brockport State College and masters and Ph.D. degrees in school administration from Cornell University. Dr. Vallely has been acknowledged nationally for his scholarly research, receiving the American Association of School Administrator's (AASA) Finnis E. Engleman Award and the Marvin and Ruth Glock Award for the most outstanding doctoral dissertation from Cornell University. He has been acknowledged as a school administrator with the New York State Data Analysis Technical Assistance Group Excellence in Education Award and the Western New York Principal's Award for Excellence. He resides in Lancaster, NY with his wife, three daughters and son.

Be sure to visit

theEDUedge.com

for additional resources including:

- Rich information and discussion for aspiring teachers via The EDU Edge Blog, Facebook® and Twitter® communities.

- Ebook outlets for this text including Kindle®, Nook®, SONY Reader®, Kobo®, Copia® and more.

- Audiobook outlets for this text including CDbaby®, iTunes®, Amazon MP3® and more.

- Information on bulk purchase discounts, presentations by the authors and other services.